STORY

AMY JEFFS

STORYLAND

Discover the
MAGICAL MYTHS
and LOST LEGENDS
of Britain

wren
&rook

FOR ROSA-MAE

First published in Great Britain in 2023 by Wren & Rook

ISBN: 978 1 5263 6617 7
Exclusive Signed Edition: 978 1 5263 6663 4

1 3 5 7 9 10 8 6 4 2

MIX
Paper from
responsible sources
FSC
www.fsc.org   FSC® C104740

Wren & Rook
An imprint of
Hachette Children's Group
Part of Hodder & Stoughton
Carmelite House
50 Victoria Embankment
London EC4Y 0DZ

An Hachette UK Company
www.hachette.co.uk
www.hachettechildrens.co.uk

Printed and bound in Great Britain by Clays Ltd, Elcograf S.p.A.

Contents

STORIES ON THE WALLS

The year is about 1400 and you have been sent away from home to live in a castle. It's not a punishment. **You were born into a noble family**, so your parents have placed you with another family and their children, as well as several other foster children like yourself, in the hope that you will make important friends and get a good education. So far it hasn't been too bad.

The **textures and smells of your life** come from the **stone, wood, bone, pottery, leather, linen and wool** that surround you. Precious objects in the household give you glimpses of ivory, gold, silver, silk and velvet. It's a beautiful and exciting place to live, although it's cold in winter. Still, you're **lucky**; there are servants who go out for you in the bitter weather to collect timber from the barns and light your fires. And in summer, you don't mind being woken up early for your lessons, because the singing of wild birds at dawn, the cooing of the doves in the dovecote and crowing of the cockerels in the yard make the castle feel as though it has been besieged by a feathery choir.

There is a **religious man**, called a cleric, with a circle shaved into the top of his head, who also lives in this house and who teaches you and the other children to read in your mother tongue, as well as in basic Latin. With him you learn other subjects too, like geometry and music. If you are a boy, another instructor will teach you horse-riding, sword-fighting and jousting, to prepare you for your career as a knight. If you are a girl, you'll probably be made to practise embroidery, account-keeping and household management. It's possible that the division of these activities suits you perfectly, but if not, then you may find yourself looking longingly out the window each day, wishing you were a boy, jousting against straw bales, or you might catch yourself gazing up at the castle from your horse, thinking of the fine needlework skills you would be learning inside if you were a girl. **When you grow up, it's hoped you will become a knight or the wife of a knight**. If neither of these works for you at all, you may choose to have your head shaved like the cleric and join a

monastery, or you might put on a head covering and veil
and become a nun. These religious lives may well give you
more freedom and independence than any of the others
you might choose from.

When evening falls, the household comes together
to eat dinner. Usually that consists of meat caught or
reared on the grounds: perhaps pigeon pie with a savoury
pudding made of peas and poached fruit. The cook is fond
of seasoning the dishes with ingredients like almonds and
garlic. On Fridays, you have fish. After that, everyone
settles down for a story. **Stories are an important part
of life with your foster family**. They are not only read
aloud from books; they are memorised and recited by
the cleric and they decorate the walls as paintings on the
plaster or brightly coloured tapestries. You know about
the Siege of Antioch and the Fall of Troy, because you
walk past their depictions on the way to your bedroom.
You could tell your own version of the Norman Conquest
of England in 1066, because it's told in vibrant, crowded
pictures in your favourite book. The martyrdom of the
great scholar St Catherine, not all that much older than
you when she outwitted all the philosophers in the Roman
Empire, is on the walls of the chapel. Nearly all the
children in the castle agree that the best stories are full of

battles, adventure and descriptions of armour and siege machinery, as well as giants, monsters and daring women from distant lands.

Opening a book chest, the cleric brings out the *Brut Chronicle* – the story of the origins of Britain, named after Brutus, Britain's founding father. You and the other children make yourselves comfortable. It's still summer, so you decide to take your place on a window seat. This way, as you listen to the cleric read, you can look out the window and watch the twilight deepen. In the grounds beyond the castle, there is an ancient oak tree. **Then something strange happens.** Is it a trick of the half-light, or did it just bow its canopy towards you, almost as if it were not an oak tree at all, but a great, gnarled giant, watching you in return?

THIS BOOK

As a historian, I am allowed to go into libraries and hold thousand-year-old manuscripts in my hands. Sometimes their pages **smell of fires from which they were only just saved**. Sometimes they hold **secret messages from people whose experiences would otherwise have been forgotten**. I feel deeply, wildly lucky to be a historian.

Being a historian means that when someone says, 'This is what happened,' you're professionally obliged to ask questions like, **'Why?'** and **'What else was going on?'** In fact, you can ask them whether or not you're a historian. Such questions lead you to other stories and, I guarantee it, make you a wiser human.

At the same time, a big part of being a historian is working out *when* things happened. This book tells stories written down in the Middle Ages or medieval period. In

Britain, this sits between the departure of the Romans in 410 *Anno Domini* or AD (that is, 410 years after Christ was born – *Anno Domini* is Latin for 'the Year of our Lord') and around 1500 AD, when Tudor figures like Henry VIII took centre stage. That being said, the stories are often set many hundreds of years earlier than the Middle Ages. These stories are myths and legends, which brings me to another part of being a historian.

History has a lot to do with separating **real past events from made-up ones**. But this book is *about* the made-up ones and how they helped shape the real ones. I will therefore follow each myth or legend with a few lines of history. But there is always a bit of myth in history, as well as the other way round. All that we really have is the surviving evidence: things like texts, pictures, pottery shards, letters, old weapons, skeletons and monuments. **History is no more or less than a case put together from that evidence.**

But that's enough explanation for now. Let's put on our

medieval goggles and look at an ancient map.

Since Creation, which is when the world was thought to have been created by God, a cluster of islands has been lying undiscovered at the western edge of Europe, Asia and Africa – the edge of the world by medieval European reckoning. Winters and summers have come and gone and many generations of animals, fish and birds have thrived. The islands are completely empty of humans.

But everything is about to change. Their story is about to begin.

In the place marked 'Syria', near the middle of the medieval map, thirty ambitious, unusually tall sisters have been discovered on the brink of an act of terrible treason. Now, their punishment is as cruel as the crime they planned. They have been cast adrift on a stormy sea and they are surely doomed. But their fate is tied to the biggest of the distant islands and the wind is driving them furiously, relentlessly, west . . .

THE THIRTY SISTERS

WHY BRITAIN WAS ONCE CALLED ALBION

The boat pitched and dived on black waves that slammed against the hull like the bodies of sea monsters. Meanwhile, inside the boat, the sisters clung to each other and gritted their teeth. Only a few days ago they had been queens in coloured silks, with carefully woven hair and pearls dangling from their earlobes, but now that life was gone. Now, curled together, surrounded by the stench of the boat's belly, they would be lucky to survive till morning. The older sisters sang songs to distract the younger ones from thoughts of splintering wood and the rush of dark water. The songs also helped them forget their fear – all except Albina, **who felt not fear but anger**.

Albina was the eldest of the sisters and she had brought them to this. Only a few days ago, in the bright Syrian sunshine, she had sat them all underneath a spreading fig tree and reminded them of the shame of their situation. They were the wives of their royal father's thirty closest barons, who were all kings in their own right. She and her sisters were no better off than slaves.

'Look how strong we are,' she said to her sisters, 'look how wise. And yet we serve our husbands. **We should be the ones ruling them!'**

Then Albina told her sisters to kill their husbands: 'Tonight, when they have fallen asleep.'

The sisters all liked the plan, except the youngest, who only pretended to. She secretly loved her husband and did not want him to die. When she went to bed that night, she told him straightaway what Albina had said. They went to her father and told him everything.

Without delay, the King seized his daughters and had them all stand trial. **Their guilt was obvious**, their protests pointless in the face of the treason they had been ready to commit. The King kept his youngest daughter back, but the rest of his daughters were taken to a harbour where his guards threw them into the hull of a boat without a rudder. As the vessel was cut free, the wind filled its sails and carried them away. They sat in the dark as the hours passed, listening to the winds rising, the rain starting to fall and the waters beginning to churn. As the storm raged, Albina sat and seethed, furious with her treacherous sister and full of ambition despite the desperation of their plight.

The storm continued for three nights, but when the third morning dawned, the sisters awoke to the sound of waves breaking on the beach and gulls laughing over the breeze. Following Albina out of the hull and into the daylight, the women found their boat had washed up on a beach that ran between the sea and cliffs of pure white stone. Albina, so determined to be first on the land she forgot how weak the journey had made her, jumped over the rails of the boat. As soon as her feet touched the shingle, she picked up a handful of stones. Then she strode off up the beach. Behind her, her sisters dropped,

one by one, from the stranded vessel. They stumbled over the rocks after Albina, who had reached a path leading up to the headland. From there, they made for a forest and found blackberries. Elsewhere there were pears, chestnuts and wild garlic. **They ate hungrily. Then they slept. Slowly their strength returned.**

In the days and weeks that followed, they began to explore. They wandered far and wide, but nowhere – not in forests or valleys, plains or mountains – did they find a plume of smoke or a human footprint. The land appeared empty. When it was clear the island was empty of inhabitants, Albina said, 'I propose we claim this land. **I propose you name me queen.** If you object, then you should tell me now.'

Not one of the sisters spoke, so she continued, 'My name is Albina, so **let's call this place Albion.** Let's live here and rule as we intended to do in Syria.'

Now that they were sure they would not find anyone else to help them, the sisters knew they must learn to thrive. There had never before been anyone in Albion to hunt the birds, animals and fish, so the skies, forests and rivers were teeming with life. What the sisters knew of working fibres from childhood hours weaving cloth, they applied to **making nets from the stems of nettles,**

as well as rope and baskets. What they knew of courtly hunting, they applied to **catching hare and deer**, and they fashioned snares to trap their prey. What they knew of sewing and fine leatherwork, they applied to **making supple and warm clothes** in which they could run, hunt and sleep. Over the years, they worked, devised, invented and grew strong. Having been princesses who knew nothing but comfort and finery, they became hardened to wind, rain and cold. **They became wild and absolutely free.**

The sisters were much happier on Albion than they had ever been before. They were well fed and independent, and their home was full of beauty. **But what would happen when they died? Who would there be to remember them?** Each of them asked herself such questions every now and then, but one night it happened that they all asked it in their minds at the same time. As they lay around the fire, their feelings flowed together and billowed into one great beacon. To us it would have been neither visible nor audible, but it penetrated deep into the earth, into the very **abyss of Hell**. There, it attracted the attention of the demons. They rose to the surface of the earth and found the women sleeping. When the sisters woke up, they were **pregnant**. Nine months later, a race of giants, **half-human, half-demon**, was born.

For over sixty years the giants of Albion ruled the land, building great dwellings on the hills and forging treasures from the metals that ran in Albion's veins. They were private creatures, who preferred **solitude in hollows and hills** to the company of others, but they were also proud of their queenly mothers and would defend Albion to the last.

So it was that after sixty years had passed, one of Albina's gigantic children told his mother's story with fierce dignity. He staked his claim to the land, even though the ropes that now bound him crushed his great knees against his chest and clamped his fists over his massive, swivelling eyes. He was a prisoner of the Trojans, and the corpses of his kin were strewn along the coast. **His name was Gogmagog . . .**

History

This story explains how the island we now call Britain received its first name – Albion – and came to be inhabited by giants. The myth comes from an anonymous medieval poem called **'Of the Great Giants'**, but surely the story was seen as fantasy? Did these educated medieval people really believe in giants? Today, we might think of them as fantastical creatures, but a person in medieval times would have told you that giants were once as common as the mountains and hills. It's a belief rooted in Jewish and Christian scripture, which says that **giants were the children of human women and fallen angels, or demons**, expelled from heaven at the very dawn of time.

'Of the Great Giants' ends by saying that the giants of Albion were responsible for creating the huge ruins now found in Britain's landscape. Perhaps the author was thinking of Iron Age hill forts, like those of Maiden Castle and South Cadbury. Were these once the castles and encampments of Albina's children? Could they be the work of giants?

THE GODDESS SPEAKS

HOW BRITAIN GOT ITS NAME, AND THE ORIGINS OF THE WELSH

There's a legend of how the Greek army once breached the gates of a city called Troy by hiding inside a huge wooden horse. The Trojans thought the horse had been left behind by the retreating Greek army, so brought it inside the city walls. When night fell, the Greeks climbed out of the horse and let in the rest of the army, which had only pretended to retreat. Those Trojans who managed to escape death or capture by the Greeks fled. They were led to Italy by Aeneas, a **son of the goddess Venus**, where he established a city that would one day be called Rome.

About thirteen hundred years before Christ (BC), Brutus, the great grandson of Aeneas, was born. When he grew up, he killed his father in a hunting accident. For this, he was banished. Alone in a small boat, roaming the Mediterranean, he longed to both find a home and prove himself. The opportunity came when he moored his boat in a city ruled by the Greek King Pandrasus. There, Brutus discovered thousands of **enslaved Trojans who had never managed to escape the Greeks**. As a descendant of the goddess Venus, he had a way of inspiring people's loyalty. Speaking with the Trojan slaves, he convinced them of their right to freedom and led them in an uprising.

After the revolt, King Pandrasus offered Brutus his daughter Inogen's hand in marriage, as well as a fleet of ships and chests full of gold. He was desperate for Brutus and the Trojans to leave. As they sailed away, **Inogen cried until she had no more tears**, but Brutus was happy; he had a wife and loyal followers; he had wealth and transport. **All he needed now was to find a homeland.**

Brutus and the Trojans wandered and wandered, finding nowhere to settle. As the weeks passed, Brutus felt himself becoming increasingly frustrated, even desperate. One evening, he docked his fleet at a quiet island called Logice and found a long-abandoned temple dedicated to the goddess Diana. There, Brutus chose twelve of his most trusted soldiers to perform a ritual sacrifice with him before a statue of the goddess. Perhaps she would give him a sign.

As night fell, the men chased and killed a beautiful white stag, cutting its throat, draining its dark blood into a bowl and mingling it with wine. Four times Brutus circled the altar before the idol of the goddess, pouring the offering into a fire burning on the altar.

Then, nine times Brutus cried: 'Forest goddess, terror of beasts, power in the heights and in the deeps, reveal our destined homeland!'

After that, Brutus laid his dark head down on the white stag's skin and fell asleep in front of the statue. At once, **the stone goddess's eyes opened wide**.

Diana was moved. Not for centuries had anyone worshipped her here. When the ships had docked, her mind had nodded towards the noise. When the men had entered the temple, she had felt a longing in her heart. When their leader had made his sacrifice, spoken words of worship, danced around the altar, she had awoken. Only once Brutus and his men were asleep did she move.

Brutus's dark form lay curled on the white pelt of the stag. *Yes*, she thought, *I see Venus in the curve of those lips and the glow of that skin*. He is her making. Diana put her hands out and pierced Brutus's sleeping mind, felt around it with her fingers, caught at the nerves and sent pulses through them. She felt the heat of his ambition

flooding her stone-cold limbs, the fierceness of his determination charging her veins with life. Diana **drank in the strength of this sinuous, dancing youth and, adding it to her own,** towered over him, billowing up like white smoke from a bonfire.

That night, Brutus dreamed he saw the statue of Diana come to life, swelling in the firelight to a vast and terrible size. Her marble shoulders were muscular from the draw of the bow, and her face glared with the sharp focus of a hunter. As her lips parted, he heard her speak in a voice like crackling flames:

'Brutus! In the western ocean is an island. Giants live there now, but it will become your home. There you will build a New Troy and found a royal line to rule the round circle of the earth.'

And as she cried her **prophecy**, she flung out her veined stone hand to the west, to the place where, just hours before, the sun had set. At this, Brutus awoke.

He lay in the dawn light, the brightness of her still burning his eyes. Before him, the statue stood motionless, its eyes blank. Waking the men, he shared the vision and they returned to the ships, determined. 'Who's afraid of a few far-off giants?' they said. Within the statue, the spirit of Diana grew cold.

The journey to Albion took Brutus between the Pillars of Hercules, the two mountains either side of the entrance to the Great Ocean. Then, though their ships nearly sank with the effort, the Trojans resisted the song of the sirens. They had heard stories of how these women, by singing on their lonely rock, had lured many sailors to their deaths.

As the Trojan ships sailed north on the Great Ocean, they visited Gaul to raid for supplies. There they met more Trojans led by a warlord called Corineus. He was a **famous giant-killer** and the goddess had warned them about giants. Brutus invited Corineus to join his fleet. On they sailed until they spied cliffs on the western horizon. Brutus, knowing that this must be the place described by Diana, directed his fleet towards the coast. They rowed up the mouth of a river and made camp.

That night, by the light of a dancing fire, Brutus told his companions that he would name this land Britain after himself. He said he would **divide Britain's regions between his closest men** and Corineus would be lord of the region to the west, which would be called Cornwall in his honour. Now all they had to do was defeat the giants.

But Albina and her sisters' children had an instinct for danger and retreated within their hill forts, or hid in caves and hollows, burying their ancestral treasures. Only when the Trojans held a festival beside the sea, and were all gathered in one place, did they finally strike.

The day was radiant, the sky was thrush-egg blue, the sea sparkled, the people sang, and twenty giants crept over the headland. One was thin and grey as a fenland eel, another gorse-haired and bracken-red as the western mountains, and yet another was white and undulating as the chalk downlands to the south. Beside them, their leader was like a boulder among pebbles. Gogmagog, it was said, could uproot an oak tree as if it were a twig of hazel.

When Corineus and Brutus saw the giants on the

cliffs, they shouted to their soldiers, who went nowhere unarmed. The men swarmed up the cliff paths with the speed of stinging insects. And though the giants were huge and strong, the Trojans were organised and experienced in battle. Before the sun had started to set, **all the giants of Albion had been killed**. All, that is, **except one**.

In the salt spray from the ocean, the soldiers tied up Gogmagog on the cliffs and demanded he tell them how his kind had come to Britain. He spat. This land was Albion, named by his mother, Queen Albina. It would never have another name.

Then Gogmagog told the Trojans he owned Albion; it was *his* land, inherited from Albina, the first person to ever set foot on its shores. And he told them about how she and her sisters had conceived the giants and made them their heirs. But the men who now stood before him did not care one bit and laughed. They had already built settlements along the coast and, when they had finished off Gogmagog, they would build a New Troy and rule the land forever. **The giant's words did not scare them.** They would simply be spun into stories on winter nights, to help pass the hours of darkness.

When Gogmagog had finished speaking, Brutus challenged Corineus to wrestle the giant. His friend agreed without question. Throwing down his weapons, Corineus waved his bare hands in the air. It was like the old days in Gaul.

The cheering men encircled the pair as Corineus bounced on the balls of his feet, knees bent, his fists clenching and unclenching, and Gogmagog was untied. And at once they locked together. The men's laughter became shouts of encouragement, turning gradually to fear. For all Corineus's prowess, Gogmagog had the upper hand. He girded his opponent, squeezing and squeezing, till *crack!* He broke three of Corineus's ribs.

The men were worried now. Gogmagog may have been the bigger fighter, but surely Corineus was quicker and more skilled? Surely the famous giant-killer would win? The Trojans held their breath. The only sounds were Corineus's panting grunts and the giant's hideous growls.

But they need not have worried. When Corineus heard his bones break, his anger became so acute that he found new strength. Now, he screamed, lifted the giant from the ground and charged to the edge of the cliffs. Man and giant stood against the blue, as still, for a moment, as sculpted stone. Then **Corineus hurled Gogmagog into the sea**. When the splash came, he peered over the edge. The other stunned Trojans joined him. Below, the sea-foam

was pink, the rocks were red with blood and Gogmagog was gone.

After the defeat of the giants of Albion, Brutus ruled Britain without rival. Just as the goddess had said, he built a New Troy, on the river we now call the Thames. One day that city would be renamed London. In the years that followed, Brutus's wife, Inogen, bore three sons, whom she loved very much and who provided some comfort to her in her exile. She named them **Locrin**, **Albanac** and **Kamber**. When Brutus was old and dying, he divided the territories of Britain between them: **Loegria**, **Albany** and **Kambria**. These would one day be called England, Scotland and Wales.

In those first years, when Brutus ruled Britain and Corineus was lord of Cornwall, the population swelled, speaking the Trojan tongue, or 'Crooked Greek'. They came to call themselves Britons after their king. The river where they had first docked became known as the Dart, their landing place was called Totnes and the place where Corineus threw Gogmagog into the sea was remembered as 'Gogmagog's Leap'. Later, people carved their image into the chalk of Plymouth Hoe, so perhaps the fight happened there. The picture has long since gone.

And though, after Corineus's victory, the gigantic children of Albina could no longer be found in the hollows and the hills of Albion, the name she gave her kingdom would be whispered beside many a fire when nights were dark. Thanks to the Britons' love of stories, **Albion would never be forgotten**.

History

When people in medieval Britain and Ireland wanted to know about history, they generally turned to the Bible or classical literature. This is because classical literature had circulated in the immensely wealthy Roman Empire, which had brought books all the way to Britain. It included long stories about ancient battles, called epics, such as the Fall of Troy, as well as stories about heroes, gods and monsters like Hercules, Perseus and Medusa. After 313 AD, when Christianity became the official religion of the Roman Empire, the stories in the Bible circulated just as widely.

Biblical and classical stories aren't set in Britain or Ireland, but around the Mediterranean, North Africa and the Middle East. Britain and Ireland were not near to any of them. In fact, they were as far west as it was possible to go. **They sat as lonely outposts in the sea.**

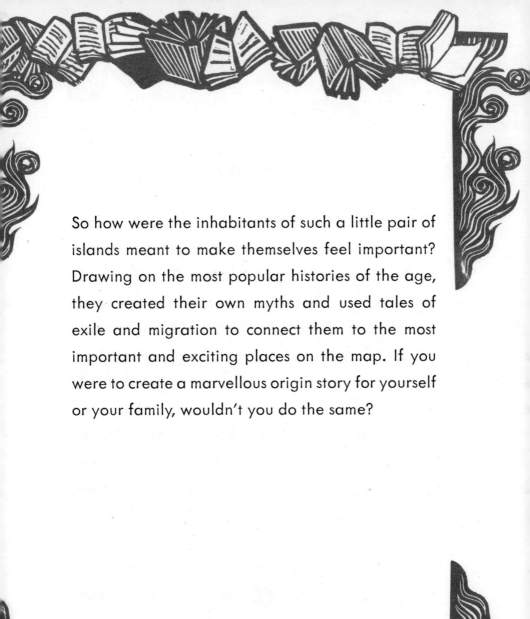

So how were the inhabitants of such a little pair of islands meant to make themselves feel important? Drawing on the most popular histories of the age, they created their own myths and used tales of exile and migration to connect them to the most important and exciting places on the map. If you were to create a marvellous origin story for yourself or your family, wouldn't you do the same?

DAUGHTER OF PHARAOH

THE ORIGINS OF THE SCOTS

S cota was in love with a Greek prince called
Gaythelos. He had won favour with Pharaoh,
Scota's father, after leading successful military
campaigns in Ethiopia. Scota did not care that
Gaythelos's own father had robbed him of royal duties due
to his stubborn independence. She married him regardless
and **her loyalty never wavered**.

They might have lived happily in the Egyptian court,
but one day, a man called Moses arrived and changed
everything. He wanted her father, the Pharaoh, to free all
the slaves they depended on for their daily needs as well
as the building of their city. Pharaoh's answer was no.
Moses asked again. Again, the answer was no. Scota and
Gaythelos felt trouble churning over the great stone palace
like storm clouds.

Moses continued to demand freedom for the slaves, but

Pharoah went on refusing. The longer Pharaoh refused, the worse things became. Plagues of lice, sickness and fire rained down on the Egyptians. The River Nile swelled with millions of frogs, which clambered and croaked into everyone's homes. **Only when the firstborn son of each Egyptian household died did Pharaoh let the slaves go.** But they had only got as far as the Red Sea when Pharaoh changed his mind and chased after them with his troops. Later that day, Scota received news that the sea had parted for the liberated slaves, letting them cross safely to the other side, but then it had crashed down over her father, drowning him and all his soldiers. The slaves escaped and began journeying across the desert to the east, in search of a homeland. In the city, unrest seethed. Scota and Gaythelos made up their minds to leave.

The pair gathered a following of Greek and Egyptian nobles and set sail on the Nile. While the slaves, who were called the Israelites, wandered east, Scota and Gaythelos went north. They entered the Mediterranean Sea, then, passing between the two towering pillars of Hercules, they resisted the song of the sirens and tracked the coastline north, docking in Spain. There they set about building a new city and called it Brigantia, though today its name is A Coruña.

But they had settled too soon. Not long after their arrival in Spain, local tribes tried to overthrow them. Rather than give in, Scota and Gaythelos built high walls and a great watchtower with views across land and sea. Later it was said to have been built by Hercules, but that is just a story.

For decades, though their defences withstood local armies, Scota and Gaythelos's people never knew true peace. The local tribes said they would leave them alone in exchange for gold and slaves, but they refused to submit. **What they needed was a land of their own**, but by now they were getting too old to take to their ships and go

wandering. They sent their sons off to explore; their names were Hiber and Hymec. The pair went willingly, sailing west and docking on all the dry land they found, hoping against hope for success. _

When the brothers finally arrived home from their expedition, they were greeted with troubled faces. Gaythelos was dying. Hiber and Hymec rushed to his side. Scota was sitting at his bedside, proud and still.

They took their father's hands and began to tell him about an island they had found, with green mountains and quiet coves, wide fish-filled rivers and fertile fields. They said that the small communities that lived there were no match for their own armies. This would become their homeland. **This is where they would be free.**

Gaythelos gathered his strength and spoke up in a frail voice: 'The gods have kept us safe here and now they are showing us the way to a new home. **Go**. Found a new kingdom on this land. There is nothing more precious than a nation that has chosen to serve its own king, who rules by hereditary right.'

Scota remained at her husband's side as he died and she never left Brigantia, but Hiber and Hymec did as he said. They led a fleet to the island, jewel-bright in the blue sea. Once ashore, they overthrew the small local tribes and began establishing a settlement. They called themselves the Scotti, after their beloved queen. The language they spoke was called Gaelic, after Gaythelos. Then Hiber made such frequent crossings between Spain and the island that he gave his name to the Iberian Sea, the peninsula of Iberia, the River Ebro and even the island itself, which came to be called Hibernia, though now we call it Ireland.

Many centuries later, the Scotti would cross the sea to northern Britain and, after establishing a kingdom there, would continue prizing freedom above all other things. They would come to be called the Scots.

History

In the late thirteenth century, the medieval kings of England had begun insisting that they should be overlords of the kings of Scotland. They said that Brutus's eldest son Locrin, who had received the territory that would become England, was the rightful overlord of his younger brothers, Albanac and Kamber, who had received the territories that would one day be Scotland and Wales. In medieval society, the eldest brother ruled the roost. As a successor of the eldest son, the English king would therefore be able to name Scotland among his territories and demand tribute from its people.

Of course, the **Scots were outraged.** They didn't care about Locrin, or any other heir of Brutus. They got to work copying and sharing their own origin myth, which was derived from earlier Irish manuscripts. It said that they were descendants of Scota and Gaythelos, who had travelled from Egypt via Spain and settled Hibernia (modern-day

Ireland). From there, they had crossed into northern Britain and taken that territory by force. They had won it as conquerors, and, try as the English kings might to coerce them into submission, they would never accept foreign rule.

COLD PROPHECIES IN A HOT LAND

THE ORIGINS OF THE ENGLISH

S if, Queen of Thrace, was having a vision of a child sleeping in his cradle, while the towers of her own sunlit city shimmered beyond the palace window.

Then she saw the same child playing in the golden gardens below.

And now, the visions shifted before her eyes and she saw him as a pale adolescent, seated with the shamans, burning incense, lost in spells. And now she saw him as a man, leaving Thrace with his wife and people, crossing mountains, penetrating luminous lands and entering forests that towered over the black lakes and the thick-furred beasts who watched from the shadows. Sif recognised it as her own northern homeland.

Then the visions changed again. She saw the same man,

wrapped in a long grey cloak, walking alone through dark pines, the ground white with snow that was whipped up by a roaring wind.

Next she saw him climbing a leafless tree and letting himself fall.

And as she watched the sun's reflection in his blue eyes, **she thought he would surely die**. How could he survive?

But she came to understand that this could be no ordinary man, for nine times the sun set and his eyes remained bright and alive. And all around him the wind howled like a wolf, till on the ninth night he hit the forest floor and fell between the roots of the tree. Screaming, he crashed beyond the snow, into the bedrock and down to the churning waters beneath. There, three old women swam to him and took out one of his eyes.

As the old women retreated, strange letters shone from the water and he drank them in, becoming wiser than any human should be.

And now Sif saw the man on a throne, with a raven on each shoulder. Before him, feasting warriors **raised a toast** in his honour: 'To Woden!'

One of his eyes was missing, but the other shone with a strange, luminous brightness. His beard flowed to his lap

and he held in his hand a sprouting plant. Either side of him stood his seven sons, all with the same sapphire blue eyes. And each of the sons was speaking, listing the names of their own sons and their sons' sons and the kingdoms they would one day rule. At first the noise of all their voices confused Sif, but soon she began to understand single words, then a few phrases. *Wectam, son of Woden, fathered Hengist, first king of Kent. Beldig, son of Woden, fathered Idam, first king of Bernicia*, and more: kingdom after kingdom.

Sif woke up from her vision with a gasp.

She knew she had seen the future. Should she tell Thor, her husband? No. He would not understand. Thor was a strong warrior, but had no ear for prophecy.

Thor was the one who had brought her to this hot southern land, but she had grown up in the north, where even summers were cold. Now she had seen that the north was the place to which the one called Woden would return and gain wisdom through a magical sacrifice. But he had come from Thrace and his blue eyes were the same as her own. He was one of her children's children.

She shuddered as she remembered how he would fall deep under the tree into the water under its roots. Thanks to the wisdom he gained there, he would become a great king in the north. He would father seven sons, whose own descendants would be rulers.

If Sif had seen further into the prophecy, she would have known even more. She would have known that the descendent called Hengist would be one of the first to arrive in Britain, where he would charm the cowardly British king. Receiving lands from him in exchange for service, Hengist would establish a kingdom in Kent. The territory of the Britons, which had once covered the whole island, would slowly be lost to a new power. And the future English would begin to settle the land.

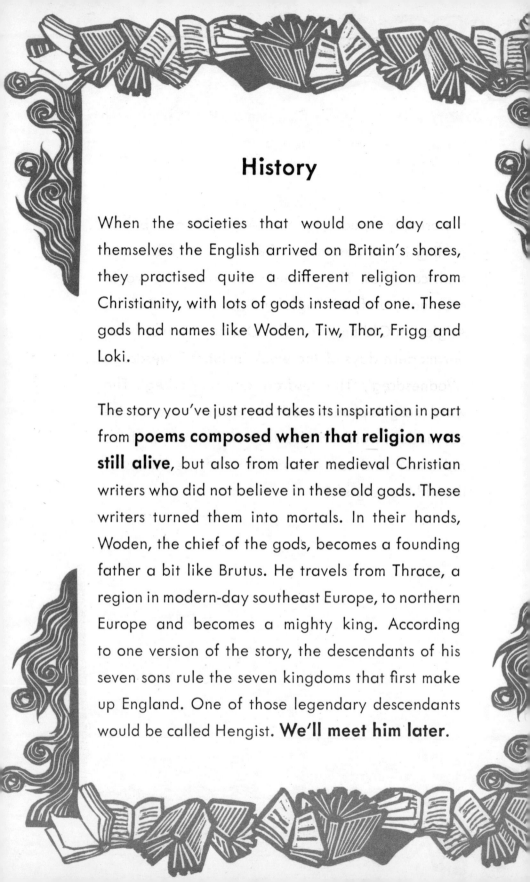

History

When the societies that would one day call themselves the English arrived on Britain's shores, they practised quite a different religion from Christianity, with lots of gods instead of one. These gods had names like Woden, Tiw, Thor, Frigg and Loki.

The story you've just read takes its inspiration in part from **poems composed when that religion was still alive**, but also from later medieval Christian writers who did not believe in these old gods. These writers turned them into mortals. In their hands, Woden, the chief of the gods, becomes a founding father a bit like Brutus. He travels from Thrace, a region in modern-day southeast Europe, to northern Europe and becomes a mighty king. According to one version of the story, the descendants of his seven sons rule the seven kingdoms that first make up England. One of those legendary descendants would be called Hengist. **We'll meet him later.**

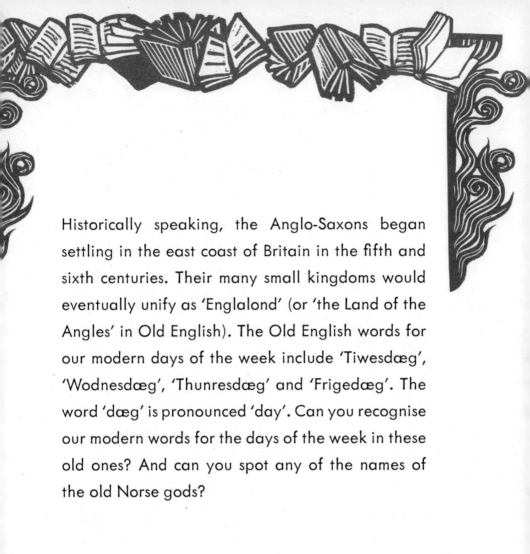

Historically speaking, the Anglo-Saxons began settling in the east coast of Britain in the fifth and sixth centuries. Their many small kingdoms would eventually unify as 'Englalond' (or 'the Land of the Angles' in Old English). The Old English words for our modern days of the week include 'Tiwesdæg', 'Wodnesdæg', 'Thunresdæg' and 'Frigedæg'. The word 'dæg' is pronounced 'day'. Can you recognise our modern words for the days of the week in these old ones? And can you spot any of the names of the old Norse gods?

THE GIRL WHO WAS AFRAID OF THE LIGHT

HOW THE HUMBER AND THE SEVERN GOT THEIR NAMES

From the hull of the ship, Estrildis could hear the confusing, awful sounds of the battle raging on the plains beside the river. From what she had understood of the guards' conversations, King Humber, her captor and kidnapper, had now invaded Albany, Britain's northern kingdom. During the invasion, Humber had killed Albany's King Albanac, and all the people had fled south. At this, Locrin, ruler of Loegria, had called on his brother Kamber, who ruled a realm called Kambria. They had brought their troops north to avenge Albanac and expel Humber from the island. Estrildis wanted Humber to die. Once she had been a princess in Germany, but Humber had murdered her family and taken her away. She rested her head against the sharp-smelling wood of the ship's hull and prayed for his defeat.

Outside, in the wind off the sea, the armies had met on the banks of an estuary. It was, as yet, unnamed and flanked by salt marshes usually green with the salty spires of herbs, but now turning red with blood. Locrin and Kamber had the upper hand and were beating Humber's army back into the waters. As his men struggled around him, **Humber saw he had no way of returning to the shore without being cut down by the enemy troops**. Rather than suffer this shame, he waded further into the river, his chain mail weighing him down. As the tide rose and his feet left the ground, his head slipped below the water and he drowned. From that day to this, that estuary has been called the Humber.

Once Humber had died and the victory had gone to Kamber and Locrin, the Britons searched his ships for treasure. They found Estrildis, the German princess, sitting in the hull.

'Is Humber dead?' she asked, but **no one understood** her language.

If Estrildis had hoped for freedom, she did not get it. As soon as Locrin saw her, he wanted her (it did not occur to him to ask if she wanted him in return). But fulfilling his desire would not be easy. He was Brutus's son, recently betrothed to Gwendolen, daughter of Corineus, who had killed the giant Gogmagog. Neither Gwendolen nor Corineus were the kind of people you wanted to betray. As soon as he could, Locrin took Estrildis back to New Troy and hid her in a special cave under the city. In the meantime, he married Gwendolen.

For seven years, Estrildis was imprisoned in the dark of the caves under the city. **She mourned her old life**, when she had been free to explore the forests of Germany and sail the glittering Rhine. She was sadder still when she discovered that she was pregnant. How could she raise a child down here? What was there in the darkness to nourish an infant?

When the baby was born, she called her Sabrina and, as she grew, Estrildis sang to her about the world above: about how there were such things as plants, which held their palms up to the sun and drank in the light, and birds, which wheeled and sang in open skies. **All these things filled Sabrina with wonder**, but there was something that Estrildis, in her fury and resentment, did not understand. Sabrina, knowing nothing else, had started to find delight in the caves. There were hibernating bats with soft, snub-nosed faces poking from between their wings. There were caverns in which her voice echoed off far-off walls, and narrow, knobbled passageways in which she climbed, clambered and slid. To her, the darkness was home.

Sabrina was seven years old when Corineus died and Locrin decided to bring her and Estrildis into the light. He ended his marriage to Gwendolen and declared his love for his secret bride. But he had underestimated how much Estrildis hated him for what he had done to their child and how scared she was about what would happen now.

In the privacy of her thoughts, Estrildis thought Locrin a **dangerous fool**. What did he think would happen? Gwendolen was every bit the daughter of the man who had wrestled the giant Gogmagog and thrown him into the sea. She would never submit to this betrayal without a fight. And couldn't Locrin see how her beloved Sabrina held her hands to her face when they were brought into the sunlit city, how she clung to her mother and wept if she was separated from her for even a moment? Estrildis did not see how Sabrina could ever be well after her long years in lonely shadow. For all this, Estrildis blamed and despised Locrin.

After the divorce, Gwendolen returned to her father's

domain, the Duchy of Cornwall, mustered an army and declared war against Locrin. He rode out to meet her near the River Stour and **hardly had time to utter his battle cry** before being struck in the chest by an arrow. So it was that the daughter of Corineus killed the son of Brutus and named herself Queen of the Britons. She installed herself on the throne and decided to take her revenge on his secret wife and daughter. Such was Gwendolen's anger, she would never have listened even if Estrildis had been able to explain that she never meant her any harm.

Gwendolen had them brought to the banks of a great estuary, further south and on the other side of the land from the Humber. This estuary was in a deep and wide valley, flanked by distant ridges of hills. There, without a second thought, she had Estrildis and Sabrina thrown into the churning flood, into the thundering water, into the blackness and the cold.

And, of course, Estrildis thought that everything was lost and all her hopes finished.

Terror. Fear.

But, after that, silence. She opened her eyes and, through the gloom, **she saw her child and joy swelled in her chest.**

There in front of her was Sabrina, quite at home in the darkness, smiling with delight, glorying in the shadows she preferred to the glaring daylight. And, as **her eyes grew accustomed to the gloom**, Estrildis saw another creature beside her – an otter – and Sabrina was playing with it: twisting and turning with the current, watching the soft light make silver nets on its fur. Then she swam towards her mother, a grin on her lovely face, and Estrildis reached out her hands, realising at last that her child would be happy here in the dark. Here, where they were far away from all the anger and cruelty they had known all her life. Here, where they could be one with the creatures of the river, far from the too-bright sky. Sabrina took Estrildis's hand and led her deeper still.

In the centuries that followed, mother and child found wonders in the wandering tendrils of weeds, the blue lightning kingfishers, the long lives of eels and the strange habits of dragonfly nymphs. **They found friends among the peaceful people** who lived by the river, swam in its kinder pools and cared for its creatures, birds and fish. And the two of them made the river their home, so that it came to bear Sabrina's name, though by some corruption of speech, it is now called the Severn.

History

Many myths about the deep past of the Britons were written down around 1136. This chronicle, known as the *Brut*, after Brutus, was the most widely read history of Britain for hundreds of years. It tells us that Gwendolen ruled for fifteen years and, for all her murderous cruelty, proved to be a much more effective ruler than Locrin.

The *Brut* was written down at a time in history when the Empress Matilda, daughter of Henry I of England, was claiming the throne of England. She was the former king's direct heir, so surely it should have gone to her? However, the barons of Britain did not want a woman on the throne and so they supported the rival claim of Stephen of Blois. **He won.** The only compensation for Matilda was that her eldest son would inherit the throne after Stephen's death. The boy became King Henry II.

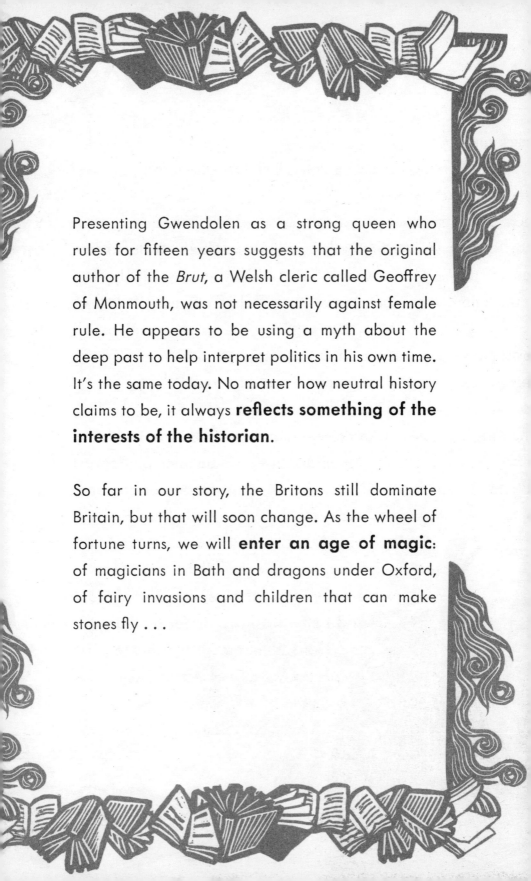

Presenting Gwendolen as a strong queen who rules for fifteen years suggests that the original author of the *Brut*, a Welsh cleric called Geoffrey of Monmouth, was not necessarily against female rule. He appears to be using a myth about the deep past to help interpret politics in his own time. It's the same today. No matter how neutral history claims to be, it always **reflects something of the interests of the historian.**

So far in our story, the Britons still dominate Britain, but that will soon change. As the wheel of fortune turns, we will **enter an age of magic**: of magicians in Bath and dragons under Oxford, of fairy invasions and children that can make stones fly . . .

THE KING WITH WINGS

THE FOUNDER OF BATH

Bladud, ruler of Britain, said he was the greatest sovereign that had ever lived, and his son Lear believed him. Why wouldn't he? Bladud was an inventor, an architect and a magician. Nine hundred years before Christ (BC), Bladud had built the city of Bath in a wooded valley, channelling warm waters into stone pools and decorating them with pillars, pediments and vaults. He had dedicated the baths to the Roman goddess Minerva and burned fires in her honour that cooled into balls of stone.

Lear also knew his father could use magic to speak with the dead. He had seen his father crouching beside the heated pools on cold nights, burning herbs, mingling the smoke from the fires with steam rising from the water.

There, in the haze, Bladud summoned dark spirits and harnessed powers to tell the future. Lear had watched in the doorway, unnoticed by his father.

Bladud taught his sinister magic to all the people in the cities and countryside, until everyone in Britain could summon the dead. It was an evil age. Bladud had found the Underworld and brought it under his sway. The power intoxicated him. He wanted more.

One day, the King announced, 'I have delved as deep as it is possible to go, but I have not yet conquered the sky. Now, to prove my greatness, I want to fly.'

That summer, as usual, Bladud took his court to the biggest city in the land, the New Troy (it was yet to be called London). He then charged his servants with gathering the feathers needed for his next invention. The young Lear went with them to the banks of the Thames, a great river where birds, mussels and fish made their homes. At the height of summer, swans regrow their plumage, shedding their old feathers on to the ground. Lear gathered armfuls from the buzzing banks, careful to choose only clean and undamaged plumes of good length. Sometimes, to reach the best ones, he would venture close to broods of cygnets and the **parents would hiss him away, baring their barbed tongues and arcing their snowy wings.**

The prince collected more feathers that day than anyone else and, as night fell, he rode proudly back in the slaves' wagon. Bladud met them outside his palace in the New Troy, nodding his approval at their load. He did not even greet his son, and soon he was turning to leave. Lear ran after him, clutching a handful of the best feathers, wanting to tell him how he had won them despite the hissing of the swans and the dangerous rushing of the river, but Bladud took his wrists in one hand and snatched the feathers with the other.

'Don't touch these,' he hissed, his teeth bared, 'you'll damage them.'

After that, Lear did not see his father for the rest of the summer, nor the whole of that autumn. Bladud shut himself away in the chamber he used for his own private studies. The slaves served him food and hushed the boy if he made too much noise. **Anxious to help his father as best he could, but longing to be close to him**, Lear played quietly in the corridor nearest the study door.

One cold, bright afternoon, Bladud finally emerged. He did not look at Lear as he strode to the stairway that led to the highest tower in the palace. He had crafted wings from the swan feathers and strapped them to his arms. **Dazzled by their size and intricacy**, Lear ran downstairs and

out into the courtyard. He wanted to see his father fly!

Bladud stepped on to the uppermost ledge of the highest tower. The wings extended from his arms, their feathers fluttering. Everywhere, the citizens stopped in the streets or looked up from barges and rafts. They could not help but wonder at what they saw, and Lear too marvelled at the silhouette of his father, whose winged arms were now open wide. When this great ambition of flying had been achieved, they would **sit together at the feast**.

Then, without warning, Bladud leapt. The watchers had known he would, and yet the act brought **a gasp from both sides of the river**. For a moment the sun caught his outline, framing him in a halo of fire. And Lear expected to see him begin to beat his arms, then rise through the air and soar up, up, up into the clear sky, becoming smaller and smaller until his was a speck against the blue. **But he did not.** Instead, one of his wings swooped underneath him and his shoulders whipped back. Instead, even as Lear brought his hands together, ready to clap and cheer, Bladud twisted round in the empty air, his **hands clutching at nothing.**

Lear watched without understanding what he was seeing. Why was his father playing this trick? Why wasn't he flying?

Bladud was falling, his wings streaming above him. Then, after several long moments, in which not one citizen breathed, the **King crashed on to the sun-warmed roof** of Apollo's temple, striking the tiles. With that, he lay still. The people put their hands to their hearts and mouths in horror as the ragged wings settled in a white V against the red tiles and a widening pool of blood. In the courtyard beside the palace, the boy did not move. He went on waiting for his father to stand, and when the slaves and guards knelt in front of him and said, **'Long live the King,'** he did not even blink.

History

You may have heard of the play *King Lear* by William Shakespeare. He didn't make up the story. It comes from much older myths about Britain, in which Lear is Bladud's son. After Bladud's death, Lear becomes king, founds the city of Leicester and, in his old age, tests his three daughters in order to decide how to divide up his riches between them. He does this by **asking which of them loves him the most.** Two of his daughters shower him with praise and flattering words, eager for his wealth, but the youngest, Cordelia, refuses to compete. She loves him as much as a daughter loves a father, she says. Not understanding, Lear banishes her and gives everything to his other daughters. But they are greedy and strip him of his riches. **Poor and ashamed, he realises that Cordelia was the one who loved him most**, after all. His father, Bladud, lost his life because of his arrogant belief that he could fly. Lear, however, realises he too is suffering because of his pride. He makes peace with Cordelia. In the medieval version of the story, unlike the one by Shakespeare, Cordelia looks after her father till he dies of old age, then she ascends to the throne of Britain and reigns for five years: a wise and judicious queen.

THE MAGICAL CATCH

AND THE FINDING OF THE STONE OF DESTINY

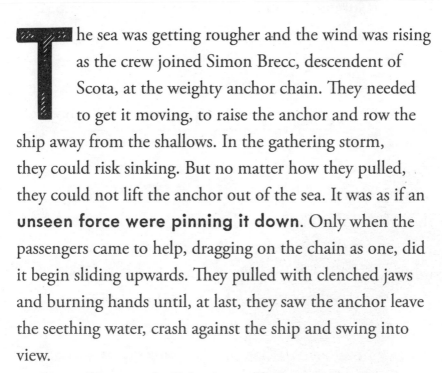

The sea was getting rougher and the wind was rising as the crew joined Simon Brecc, descendent of Scota, at the weighty anchor chain. They needed to get it moving, to raise the anchor and row the ship away from the shallows. In the gathering storm, they could risk sinking. But no matter how they pulled, they could not lift the anchor out of the sea. It was as if an **unseen force were pinning it down**. Only when the passengers came to help, dragging on the chain as one, did it begin sliding upwards. They pulled with clenched jaws and burning hands until, at last, they saw the anchor leave the seething water, crash against the ship and swing into view.

Simon Brecc and all those travelling with the fleet were the last of the Scotti to have remained in Spain since the

days of Scota and Gaythelos. But in all that time they had
never known peace from their neighbouring kingdoms.
Simon Brecc, **tired of constant war**, had resolved to
leave Spain once and for all, and travel to his homeland of
Hibernia. Except, after so long since the departure of its
first settlers, he had only a vague idea of where it lay. On
their first voyage, they had sailed too far north and found
themselves on a cluster of islands called Orkney. There they
had met Gurguint, King of the Britons, who had helped
them retrace their steps and find the land they sought.

When they had finally arrived in Hibernia, greeted by
gentle rain and a view of distant, mist-mantled mountains,
they had dropped anchor and prepared the smaller boats
to row the people ashore. But that was when the storm had
struck. Everywhere, the green waters had started turning
brown. Waves had begun rolling in from the horizon and
the light rain had become a heavy torrent. **They could
not go ashore yet after all.** That was when, with
unexpected difficulty, they had raised the heavy anchor.
Now they saw just what had been weighing it down.

A great stone object, cradled by the anchor, was hanging
in the air, even darker than the slate-grey sky, encrusted
with barnacles and garlanded with kelp. As it spun in
the pouring rain, Simon and his people discerned it to

be a **magnificent marble throne**. Despite the heaving waves, the wind and the unchecked movement of the ship, they guided it gently and set it down on the deck. It shed squirming creatures, hermit crabs and shrimp on to the sodden boards. The people inspected it, finding an intricately carved surface under the weeds, worked with lettering they could no longer read.

When Simon Brecc was finally able to make land, he brought the marble throne on to the shore. So magnificent was it, he believed it must have come from Egypt and arrived with the sons of the Egyptian princess Scota, Hymec and Hiber, the first rulers of the Scotti in Hibernia. In the days that followed, the throne was set on the Hill of Tara, which became a sacred place for the Scotti, and Simon Brecc **heard a prophecy from the gods**. It promised that wherever Scota's throne stood, the Scotti would rightfully rule.

History

Many of the myths about the origins of the Scottish have roots in earlier Irish tales. This is because the earliest Scottish settlements in northern Britain had come from Ireland. One Irish tale about a magical stone speaks of the Lia Fáil or the Stone of Destiny. In these accounts, the **stone shouts for joy when the true ruler touches it.** By the later Middle Ages, Scottish writers, especially one called Walter Bower (who died in 1449), were busy bringing together useful lore about their mythic origins to combat claims to supremacy being made by the English kings. At this time, a story took shape of a magnificent throne pulled from the seas beyond Ireland by descendants of Scota. You'll remember Scota was an ancient Egyptian princess and matriarch of the Scots, so suggesting the stone once belonged to her made it very important indeed.

The story of Simon Brecc's throne and the prophecy associated with it would have been very meaningful

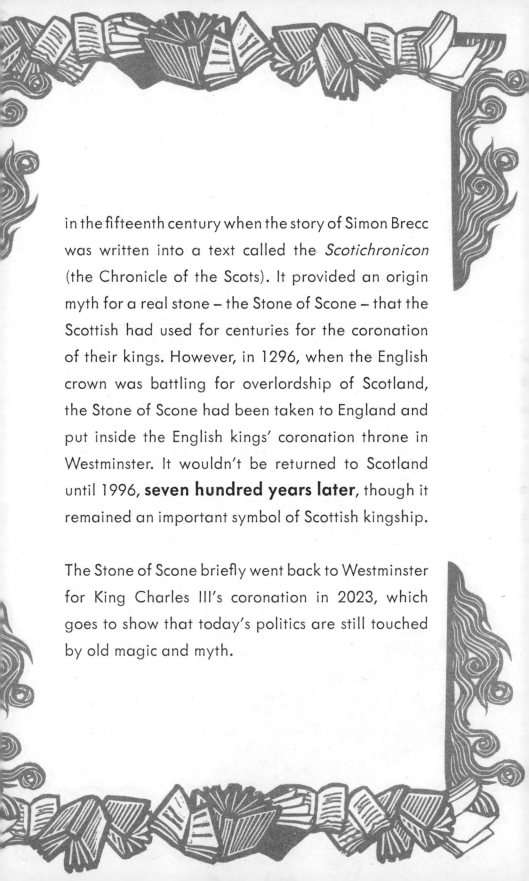

in the fifteenth century when the story of Simon Brecc was written into a text called the *Scotichronicon* (the Chronicle of the Scots). It provided an origin myth for a real stone – the Stone of Scone – that the Scottish had used for centuries for the coronation of their kings. However, in 1296, when the English crown was battling for overlordship of Scotland, the Stone of Scone had been taken to England and put inside the English kings' coronation throne in Westminster. It wouldn't be returned to Scotland until 1996, **seven hundred years later**, though it remained an important symbol of Scottish kingship.

The Stone of Scone briefly went back to Westminster for King Charles III's coronation in 2023, which goes to show that today's politics are still touched by old magic and myth.

THE FAIRIES, THE SCREAM AND THE THIEF

HOW TWO DRAGONS WERE HIDDEN IN A HILL

Lludd was a good king. He was so good and so loved by his people that they renamed New Troy after him, calling it 'London'. But Lludd's luck began to change when a **race of devious fairies** invaded, settling over the land like a mist. They might have been easy to defeat in battle, but so good was their hearing that they **eavesdropped on every plan to oust them**. The people felt the oppression of the small, spying invaders the length and breadth of the land.

But that was not the only plague being suffered by the Britons. The second was a **scream that resounded from the sky every May Day**, causing death and destruction. For several years, no women who had been pregnant on May Day were able to deliver their children and no blossoms set into fruit. Where did the scream come from? No one knew, but everyone **wished it gone**.

And if the fairies and the scream were not enough, there was a third and equally terrible blight. For years now, something or someone had been **emptying the royal food stores as soon as they were filled**, so that nothing could be shared with the poor. The King's guards sat up through the night in the barns, hoping to catch the thief, but in the mornings all they could say was that the baskets and barrels were full one moment and empty the next.

King Lludd sought advice from his wise brother Llefelys, who ruled Gaul. They met in the sea between Gaul and Britain, where they wouldn't be overheard by the fairies. Still, just in case, they **whispered to each other down the barrel of a long horn**.

At first, Lludd could hear his brother saying nothing but obscene words and insults. This was not like Llefelys at all! But then he flushed out the horn with wine and expelled a **demon that had been hiding inside**. Now Lludd listened again and, glad to hear his brother's gentle voice, learned everything he needed to know.

When the siblings had waved each other farewell, Lludd sailed silently back to the Thames. Llefelys had told him the causes of the plagues and how they could be defeated, but Lludd's tasks were not easy. Entering the mouth of the estuary, he prayed he'd be equal to the challenge.

Following his brother's advice, Lludd trapped and dried thousands of magical insects, making them into a potion. Then he called everyone to an assembly, as if to broker peace. A huge crowd gathered in one of the main squares in London and Lludd could see that nearly all the fairy race was present. **They listened eagerly for him to speak**, not knowing that there were troops concealed in the crowd with flasks of insect water

hidden in their coats. At Lludd's signal, the troops brought out the flasks and scattered the water over the people and fairies around them. While the Britons only gasped and spluttered, the **water was poison to the troublesome fairies**. When it touched them, they blistered and died. Thus the first plague was defeated, but still two more remained.

The screaming plague came that May Day as usual. Following his brother's advice, Lludd sunk a great cauldron of mead into the earth at the very centre of the land (which in those days was Oxford) and covered it with a cloth. Suddenly, a **pair of fighting dragons** appeared high up in the sky. With scaly wings slicing the air and lightning breath flashing, they clawed at each other, then they began to fall and, not seeing the cloth nor the mead beneath, disappeared into the cauldron. Once inside, they drank every last drop of the sweet liquor and turned into a pair of **sticky, sleepy pigs**.

At this, Lludd climbed into the cauldron, remembering what Llefelys had told him about the two dragons. One was a native of the land. She screamed because the other, an invader, was attacking her. He folded the cloth around the sleeping pigs. Then he hoisted them on to his back and **carried them west into the wilderness**. He crossed the Severn and reached a mountainous region called Eryri, where rain and wind swept the peaks. He passed roaring waterfalls and forded torrential streams, making for the hill called Dinas Ffaraon Dandde, or the Fort of the Fiery Pharaoh. One day it would be called Dinas Emrys, after a magical child, but we'll come back to that. Reaching the summit, Lludd saw before him a heavy grey stone beside two stone chests. He placed each of the pigs in a chest, pushed the stone away and revealed an opening in the hill.

The summit of Dinas Ffaraon Dandde was crowned with oaks so tangled it was as if they had been frozen in the act of dancing. Lush green ferns grew on their trunks and their long, sinuous boughs had caused the grass underneath them to become a deep green carpet. All was bright and full of life, except for the hole under the stone, which was dark, bare and silent.

Now that the pigs were safely locked away in their respective chests, Lludd set his back against each of the chests in turn and, his heels digging into the soft turf, pushed them into the cavernous hole. He had just enough time to heave the stone covering back over it. Then he heard the **dragons wake up and begin to roar**. Still, it was much better now. So muted was the sound that it might have been made by nothing more terrifying than the waterfalls further down the hill.

With that, Lludd travelled back to London, where the final plague awaited him. Arriving at the food stores, Lludd once again followed the advice of Llefelys. He fetched a barrel of water and sat down in the barn, which had been filled with supplies that very day. Then, as darkness fell, he waited and peered. After a while, his mind started to swim. **Strange, sleepy music started playing in his head, warmth filled his body and his eyelids began to droop.** Lludd shook his head, forcing himself to remember what to do. Taking the barrel of water, he plunged his head into it and emerged wide awake, dripping, but aware once again of his purpose. So the night went on, with the strange music and the **shock of the cold water to stop him falling asleep**. The music had been why the guards had never seen the culprit, but Llefelys had known what to do. Thanks to his brother's wisdom, Lludd remained wakeful until the thief arrived.

A giant entered the larder. He was singing to himself and carrying a wide basket on his arm. It was so big, it had been woven of whole willow trees, and he filled it as he proceeded between the piles of food, scooping up handfuls of grain, seizing whole hams and glugging from flagons of wine. Here, at last, was the source of the plague,

thought Lludd. And now he would have to defeat him.
The King stood up from his place in the corner and said in
his most commanding voice, **'Stop!'**

The gigantic thief looked over, dried peas tinkling from
his big, hairy hand. By the look on his face, he had not
expected this. **His enchantment had never yet failed**.
Normally, he would have crushed Lludd with a fist, but
he was so surprised he did not move. Then, the little man
sprang towards him. The giant batted him away, amazed,
sending Lludd sprawling into a pile of leeks. But Lludd
was not deterred. He leapt back up, drawing his sword,
and now the giant was ready. The pair fought among the
onions and grains, the hams, pies and pickles. At one
point, the giant caught Lludd so hard on the side of the
head with his basket that the King was blinded, but then
he swung his sword blindly and sliced his opponent's thigh,
causing blood to gush over a stack of smoked fish. As the
giant roared with pain, Lludd regained his vision
and ascended a pile of grain sacks. As he reached the top,
he caused it to topple and throw him forward. Then he
flung his arms out and grabbed the giant around the neck,
swiftly pressing his sword to a vein that twisted beneath the
hairy skin like a tree root under turf. The giant, for all his
size, was at last at the King's mercy.

'I surrender!' cried the giant in a voice like an underground river, 'and offer you my service if you spare my life!'

Lludd agreed and was pleased to discover that **even giants honour their oaths**. After that, the Britons were free of the terrible plagues and Lludd reigned in peace till he was old. When he died, he was buried by London's city wall, at a place ever since known as Ludgate.

History

Have you heard of *The Mabinogion*? It is the most **marvellous and mind-bending collection of Middle Welsh stories** written down in a late medieval manuscript long after they were composed. As well as King Lludd, the stories include characters like King Arthur, together with other legendary kings and queens of the Britons. There are giants and journeys to the Otherworld. There are white stags and magicians. You'll get a glimpse of another *Mabinogion* story in the chapter about King Arthur's best friend.

The tale of Lludd and the three plagues of Britain (known as 'Lludd and Llefelys') is full of wondrous scenes, such as the brothers' conversation in the English Channel down the barrel of a horn. It's also about the very real issue of **resisting invasion and occupation by foreign forces**, albeit fairies and dragons, rather than human armies. The Britons had experienced such traumas historically in the form of the Romans and the

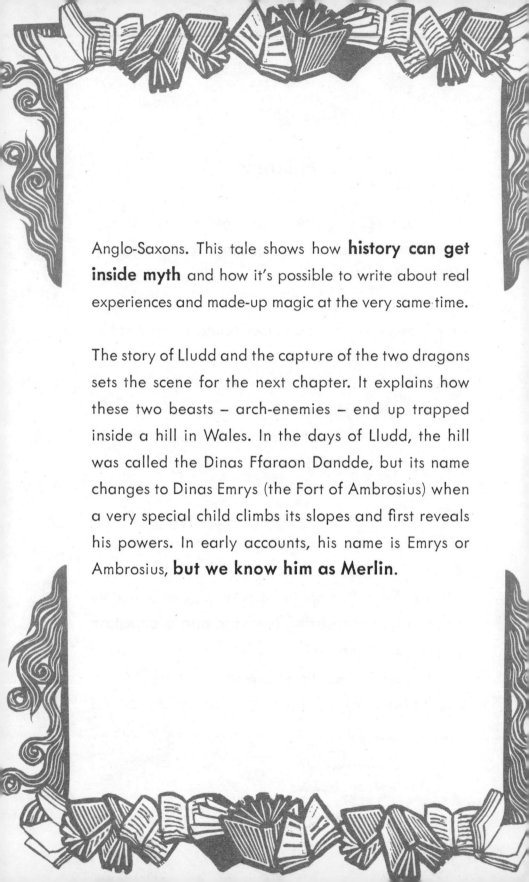

Anglo-Saxons. This tale shows how **history can get inside myth** and how it's possible to write about real experiences and made-up magic at the very same time.

The story of Lludd and the capture of the two dragons sets the scene for the next chapter. It explains how these two beasts – arch-enemies – end up trapped inside a hill in Wales. In the days of Lludd, the hill was called the Dinas Ffaraon Dandde, but its name changes to Dinas Emrys (the Fort of Ambrosius) when a very special child climbs its slopes and first reveals his powers. In early accounts, his name is Emrys or Ambrosius, **but we know him as Merlin.**

DRAGONS UNLEASHED

AND MERLIN'S FIRST PROPHECY FOR THE BRITONS

Merlin, an unusual child, was taking part in a ball game outside the walls of Carmarthen. Nearby, a troop of **colourfully dressed soldiers were resting in the sun**, tired from a long and fruitless search. They wondered if they had at last found what they were looking for, however, when the children began taunting Merlin for having no human father. One of the men stood up and walked over to the group.

'Is what you are saying about this child true?' he asked.

The children were eager to tell him everything they knew.

'Yes! Merlin's ma is a nun in the same convent as my aunty and she told my ma that his pa was a demon! Everyone here knows about it.'

When the soldier had thanked them with a handful of gold coins, he went over to Merlin, took him to his horse and lifted him into the saddle.

'Where is your mother?' he demanded.

'In the convent of St Peter.'

The soldiers found her and took her away with Merlin to the mountains. There, King Vortigern would be sitting in his tent, awaiting a child with no human father.

They reached a hill that stood apart from the others, lonely and small beside a lake, with a huge mountain behind it. As they climbed the hill, they passed waterfalls and gnarled oak trees. On the summit, there were building materials and machines. They surrounded the first courses of a stone tower, as well as a multicoloured tent, its red panels flapping, bright streamers fluttering from its roof and an armoured guard glittering at the door. This was the tent of Vortigern.

Merlin was led inside, along with his mother. **He saw the King sitting on a couch.** The man was as grey and colourless as his soldiers and tent were colourful. Once he must have been handsome, but now his eyebrows hung low and hairy over his eyes, as though his crown were far too heavy for his face. He turned towards Merlin's mother and said, 'Is it true this child has no human father?'

The scribe who stood behind the King listened to Merlin's mother's reply with a serious expression.

'When I first entered the convent,' she said, 'a handsome man used to visit me in my cell. I don't know how he got in, but he had the power to become invisible, so perhaps he had other powers too. When he was invisible, I could still feel him and hear his voice. Merlin is our child.'

The scribe, whose name was Maugantius, addressed Vortigern. 'Such a being, your majesty,' he said, 'is indeed no human, but a demon. From the very earliest ages, its kind has been known to have children with human women.'

Vortigern frowned his bushy brows, looking at the ground. Then he spoke, 'I am building a tower here to protect myself from people who want to kill me and steal my crown. But no matter how much my workers build in a day, each night the tower crumbles to the ground.'

His brows contracted yet further and his gaze wandered up towards Merlin's mother.

'My magicians have informed me that my problem will be solved by spilling the blood of a boy with no human father. Your son is such a boy.'

And now Vortigern's **gaze darted to Merlin**, who sighed a deep, knowing sigh.

'Your magicians are fools,' the child said.

Vortigern blinked at him, then recovered himself. 'What makes you say so?'

Merlin replied, 'Shouldn't they be able to tell you what's causing your tower to crumble?'

Vortigern's brow creased yet further.

'**Finding the cause is your only hope**, if you want to complete the tower,' Merlin went on. 'Have your men dig below the foundations. Then you will know what to do.'

The boy spoke with such confidence that Vortigern followed his advice. There was not much time, but he could still kill Merlin and spill all his blood if his words proved untrue. The King instructed his workers to start digging.

Rain and wind buffeted the oak trees over the days that followed. Vortigern wished the men would work faster. He felt as if his enemies must already be scaling the lower slopes of the hill. **He needed a fortress, and fast.**

The truth of the matter was that he had not received his crown according to lawful succession. In reality, Vortigern had stolen his crown.

Vortigern had once been a baron in the court of King Constantine. When the King had died, one of his three sons had stood to inherit. But the question of succession was hardly an easy one. The eldest boy's name was Constans and he was a monk, while the younger two, Aurelius and Uther, were both infants. Monks were not meant to hold the office of kingship, but neither were small children. Vortigern thought the answer was clear. **He himself should be king.**

Finding Constans to be easily led and fond of praise, Vortigern persuaded him to disregard his monastic vows and succeed his father. When the coronation day came, Constans walked to the high altar in his black monk's robes and made royal vows. As no bishops would agree to perform the ceremony, Vortigern crowned the boy himself. Of course, he did not do this for the boy's own good.

Not long afterwards, Vortigern sent a message to northern Britain, where a tribe called the Picts had their strongholds. He invited their best soldiers, paying them a handsome fee, and told Constans they would help guard against the threat of a Norwegian invasion – though, of course, no such threat existed. Constans wept piteously and thanked Vortigern for his counsel, but Vortigern had his own reasons for inviting them. Behind the back of the King, he won the Picts' loyalty by giving them gifts and inviting them to lavish feasts.

At one particularly sumptuous banquet, he made an announcement: 'The truth is, good men, that King Constans does not value us at all. He pays me barely enough to maintain my own household, let alone honour you as you deserve. This may be the last time we meet.'

The Picts shouted in outrage, calling King Constans all kinds of shameful names.

'You'd make a far better king,' they said to Vortigern, who modestly bowed his head. The next day, they murdered King Constans in cold blood, driving a dagger through his heart.

The Picts had thought the assassination would secure them a comfortable future in the court, but they had not realised Vortigern's true nature. Accusing the Picts of treason, he had them executed. Then, triumphant, Vortigern **seized the crown of Britain** and pushed it on to his head.

Aurelius and Uther, who were still infants, were taken away to safety in Brittany and the many British barons who remained loyal to them prayed they would return, one day, to reclaim their throne. Vortigern, in the meantime, resolved to protect himself as well as he could. So it was that he accepted the service of Hengist and Horsa.

When the Saxon ships docked in Kent, the men who disembarked were finely dressed, with a noble bearing. You may remember Hengist's name from Sif's vision. He could trace his lineage to Wectam, King of East Saxland, who was the eldest son of the same Woden who had traded his eye for wisdom. They had travelled to Vortigern's court, they said, because their homelands had become too crowded and they needed somewhere else to live.

Vortigern was impressed by their fine appearances, not to mention the size of their armies. Thinking their service might come in useful when Aurelius and Uther were old enough to confront him, he gave Hengist and Horsa land in Kent. Then he deepened his ties to them yet further by marrying Hengist's daughter. Her name was Ronwen.

It was during a feast that he **first glimpsed her**. He had been told she worshipped Mercury, Jupiter and Apollo, rather than the Christian God. **He was not meant to marry her**, not as a Christian king . . . and yet he found her so beautiful. When she walked the length of the hall to offer him a drink from a goblet, she greeted him in the Saxon way.

'Wassail,' she said, which meant 'be well'.

One of his servants translated for him and told him how to respond.

'Drinchail,' said Vortigern, which meant 'drink well'. Then he drank from the proffered cup. When she completed the ritual by **stepping forward and kissing him**, Vortigern's resistance crumbled away. He asked Hengist for her hand and married her that night.

Marriage can be a powerful tool. As time passed, Ronwen used her power to bring even more Saxons into Britain and she even poisoned Vortigern's son from an earlier marriage when he led the Britons in revolt.

Vortigern sought to foster peace. The Saxons' power was growing and soon Aurelius and Uther would be old enough to reclaim their titles. What if he made enemies of both sides? He therefore **invited all the British and Saxon nobles to a feast** near the town of Amesbury. It had not gone as planned. That night, the Saxons committed a most heinous act of treachery.

Many **hundreds of warriors sat together on the benches, Britons mixed up with Saxons**. Wine flowed and the night deepened, when, all of sudden, Hengist uttered a cry that would echo down the centuries:

'Seize your knives!'

At his words, the Saxons drew daggers from their waistbands and killed the Britons beside them, driving blades deep into chests and stomachs. Of the British nobles at the feast, only Vortigern and the Earl of Gloucester escaped alive. The Earl got out fighting, killing many Saxons as he went. Vortigern fled to the western mountains, far from the Saxon strongholds. There, he **began building a fortified tower**. And what with his fear of the Saxons on the one hand and Aurelius and Uther on the other, his anguish was very great. It threatened to overwhelm him even now, as he sat beside the boy with no human father, watching his men dig, and waited to discover the cause of the crumbling tower.

Below Vortigern and Merlin, one of the workers cried out. Then more cries followed, along with the splashing of rocks in water. The King and the boy saw that **a pool had been revealed at the bottom of the pit**. Taking advice from Merlin, Vortigern gave the order for the men to dig a gully and empty the pool down the hill. The dark, still hole in the summit of the hill had been filled with water since the days of Lludd. As the pool flowed away, they saw **two stone chests**. The men lifted the stone chests out of the hole and stood them side by side on the muddy ground. Then they pushed their lids away.

Merlin and Vortigern saw the **spines of two great creatures**. One spine was white, like that of a pale salamander, while the other was red, like an earthworm. Their scales were soft from long submersion, but grew hard as flint as their backs dried. Then the creatures began to writhe, lifting up their heads on long, winding necks, and snapping at the air. And suddenly the **dragons saw each other and roared**. They clawed their way out of their stone prisons.

And then their ancient battle began again. The white one charged and the red flew back, only to coil back round, snapping at the air, till the white one was forced to retreat in turn. Then, without warning and with terrible speed, the pair pushed off from the mud and **flew into the sky**.

Vortigern cowered as the twisting monsters rose, vanishing among the clouds in a blaze of sparks. Then he turned to Merlin and asked, 'What does this mean?'

Merlin shut his eyes. Within him, **a spirit that was not human began to whisper**. It told him what the dragons meant and the answer filled him with dread. Then he began to speak what he was hearing aloud to Vortigern, giving prophecies that would never be forgotten.

'The **red dragon represents the British nation**.

She will be defeated by the **white dragon, which represents the Saxons** whom you have allowed into the land. Because of the Saxons, the mountains will be made into valleys, the rivers will run with blood, the faith will be destroyed and the churches will be ruined.'

Then, sitting on the edge of the pit, **tears now flowing on his cheeks**, Merlin described many strange visions: a hedgehog hiding apples in Winchester, gold being squeezed from the leaves of stinging nettles, the red dragon weeping at the furthest edge of the drained lake, wolves with no teeth and an eagle on a mountain-top nest. These were signs of the great political events of the future. And all the while Merlin saw the white dragon attacking again and again, until there was no hope. Vortigern listened till the sun had set and the boy had fallen silent.

Then Vortigern asked in a hoarse whisper, 'How am I going to die?'

Merlin told him that, even now, Aurelius and Uther, the brothers of Constans, were travelling from Brittany to reclaim their inheritance. 'If the Saxons don't get you first, the Britons will burn you alive, trapped inside your tower.'

The very next day, **Vortigern fled**. Abandoning his unfinished tower on Dinas Ffaraon Dandde, he resorted

to a
different
stronghold, not far
from the River Wye. In
the meantime, Constans's true
heirs were indeed sailing from

Brittany to London. As Vortigern paced his remote tower, his stolen crown seeming to cut into his brow whether or not it was on his head, the bishops anointed Aurelius. They called him Ambrosius, the golden one. Then the Earl of Gloucester, who had alone of all the British barons survived the Saxon massacre at the feast, mustered an army, joined Aurelius Ambrosius and began marching west in search of Vortigern. It did not take them long to find him, for few were loyal to him now. Reaching the castle in which he hid, they surrounded its base with dry timber and threw torches on to the wood. That evening, while insects danced gold above the river and deer watched from the banks, flames spilled into the windows and caught hold of the rich furniture and many colourful hangings within.

Vortigern climbed up through the castle like a spider, reaching the battlements and stepping out into the smoky air. As he crossed the parapet, it was the **crown that hurt** first, the gold growing hot from the heat of the rising flames. It blistered his forehead, scorching a circle of skin. He glared out over the scene on the ground. The last thing Vortigern saw, beyond the brothers, beyond the army, was the small figure of the boy with no human father. King Vortigern breathed in to shout, but his lungs only filled up with smoke.

Far below, Merlin felt the gaze of the traitor strike him. He turned and walked away, into the sweet solitude of the forest.

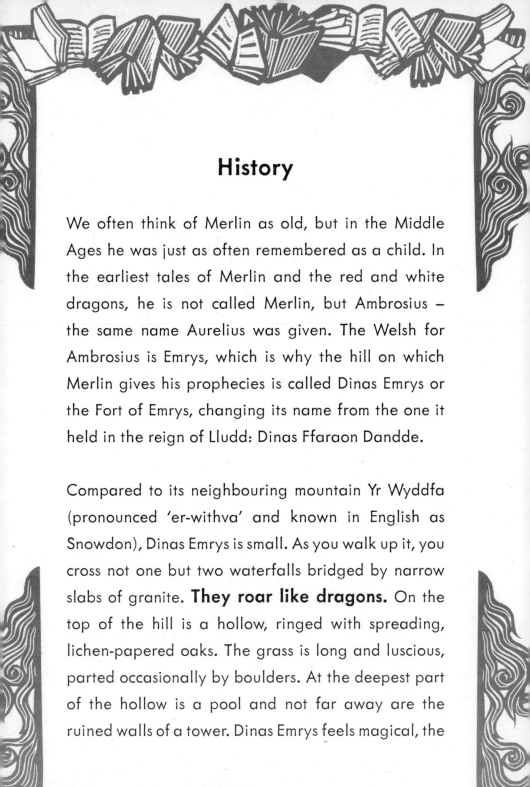

History

We often think of Merlin as old, but in the Middle Ages he was just as often remembered as a child. In the earliest tales of Merlin and the red and white dragons, he is not called Merlin, but Ambrosius – the same name Aurelius was given. The Welsh for Ambrosius is Emrys, which is why the hill on which Merlin gives his prophecies is called Dinas Emrys or the Fort of Emrys, changing its name from the one it held in the reign of Lludd: Dinas Ffaraon Dandde.

Compared to its neighbouring mountain Yr Wyddfa (pronounced 'er-withva' and known in English as Snowdon), Dinas Emrys is small. As you walk up it, you cross not one but two waterfalls bridged by narrow slabs of granite. **They roar like dragons.** On the top of the hill is a hollow, ringed with spreading, lichen-papered oaks. The grass is long and luscious, parted occasionally by boulders. At the deepest part of the hollow is a pool and not far away are the ruined walls of a tower. Dinas Emrys feels magical, the kind of place you'd expect to see a ferocious battle between two dragons. The red dragon, interpreted by Merlin as a symbol of the Britons – and later the Welsh – is still a symbol of Wales.

The myth of the red and white dragons is set at the same time as the arrival of the Saxons, led by Hengist. Years of invasion and oppression of the British would follow. This bears some resemblance to real history: the myths are set around four hundred years after the birth of Christ, which is also around the time that the Germanic tribes known as the Anglo-Saxons started crossing the North Sea in their boats and the British kingdoms began moving west.

THE GIANTS' DANCE

OR THE ORIGINS OF STONEHENGE

Only a few centuries after Creation, in the scorching regions of remotest Africa, giants were at work. This is not Africa as we know it, but imagined by people who had never seen it before. The giants abhorred the heat, not to mention each other, with **blood like lava and tempers to match**.

They were quarrying stone and they were doing so for a special purpose. The largest of them drove a wedge into a crack in the stone. She struck once, twice, three times with her hammer. When the wedge had stuck, she inserted another, striking until the crack lengthened into a long split in the rock face. Then the lump of stone, almost as big as the giant herself, groaned into her arms.

She heaved the rock on to her shoulder and walked away. **Sweat hissed from her brow** and dust dried her throat, but she journeyed without stopping for the whole of that night, pursuing the trace of a chill on the breeze. She drank deeply from rivers at daybreak and slept until sunset each day, disguised as a hill or sandbank. She did not disturb the creatures about her: herds of deer with swivelling horns, as well as beings that shaded themselves with one enormous foot or whose faces peered out from their chests. Once or twice, she saw a city, smoke rising from its rooftops, laughter and music from its streets. **Such places she avoided**. Each night she bore her load onwards, striding tirelessly on until she reached the sea.

The other giants followed with their heads bowed and their own rocks on their backs. When they came to the great ocean, they entered the water with a creak of pleasure. From here they travelled for weeks, plucking whales skywards for food. As they passed the gates of the Mediterranean, the sirens saw them and covered their beautiful mouths.

The giants waded, the heat abated and soon they had reached the part of the ocean where the clouds hung low and cold winds blew on even the warmest days. Then the lead giant saw an island and stepped from seabed to reef to cliff face and **on to the moon-illuminated meadows**. As rain began to fall, the giants made for the tallest mountain.

In later days the Irish called it Killaraus. And even later than that they said it had never existed at all. Its summit was pillowed with thyme and veiled with cloud. When the giants assembled, they were in harmony, which was unusual. **They placed the stones in circles and topped them with flatter stones.** Then they dug pits in the midst of the central circle and watched as the rain pooled into them, flowing over the rocks.

Seeing the baths were full, the giants encircled their structure in a great ring, a carol, a dance. One by one they dipped their heads below the water and all their hurts subsided. That would be enough for now. These stones had healing properties, washed into the baths by the rain.

The island was full of hollows perfectly suited to the solitary ways of giants. When they had all bathed, it was to these hollows they retreated, returning to their dance when they were wounded or sick. This was many years

ago, before that land became known as Hibernia or nearby Albion received its name. Later, there came a Great Flood in which many of the giants were swept away for good, but their healing temple endured. Later, the Scotti called it 'The Giants' Dance', perhaps because of the stately formation of its colossal stones, or perhaps because the mist preserved some memory of a unique meeting. The stones stood there for thousands of years. When at last they were moved, it was by the power of a child called Merlin.

Now, King Aurelius Ambrosius held the throne of Britain, but Merlin knew little of that. After the death of Vortigern, the boy had gone to live in a remote place called the Springs of Galabes. One part of him wanted to live among the springs forever. Another remembered the companionship of people and longed to have it back.

One day, the sound of metal – a horseshoe striking rock – cut a crimson gash through the everyday sounds Merlin had come to know. He climbed up a tree when he heard it, and saw, beneath the canopy of dark leaves, **a troop of soldiers entering the clearing on horseback.**

The soldiers called but Merlin did not answer. Then they called again, telling him they were messengers from King Aurelius. Merlin hesitated for a breath, his mind all confusion. Then he climbed

down, stepped into the clearing and agreed to go with
them to the King.

When Merlin arrived in Winchester, riding on one of
the soldiers' horses, Aurelius was standing at the city gates
with Earl Eldof of Gloucester. The young king's coiling
hair fell bronze about his shoulders and gems flashed at his
ears and fingers.

He greeted Merlin and led him into the palace. Once in
the hall, the King presented the boy with his problem.

'I want to build a fitting memorial to the Britons slaughtered by the Saxons at Vortigern's feast, but my carpenters, stonemasons and architects can think of nothing worthy.'

Merlin replied at once, 'The answer is clear; such a structure already exists. It is called the Giants' Dance and its stones are so heavy that no one living is strong enough to lift them. You'll find it on Mount Killaraus in Hibernia. If we could bring it here, then it would certainly stand forever.'

At first Aurelius laughed at the suggestion. Did they not have enough big stones in Britain? Would taking the Dance not anger the Irish king? And how would they lift them if they were so heavy? But **Merlin, annoyed by the King's laughter**, insisted that nothing else would do and that strength wasn't the only means by which they could be moved. Aurelius conceded and Merlin travelled with his army to Hibernia. Defeating the Irish king with ease, they journeyed on to Mount Killaraus.

Secretly, the King's soldiers thought the scheme ridiculous, and they frequently laughed at Merlin and teased him when Aurelius's back was turned. **Merlin refused to respond.** When they arrived at the Dance, he sat down on a mossy knoll, breathing in the scent of thyme, and invited the King's men to move the stones if they could. Now, at last, he spoke:

'We shall see which is better: brute strength or artistry and skill.'

The muscular men rocked on to their haunches, embraced the rocks or wound their hands around ropes, and, taking deep breaths, exerted their efforts on lifting the stones into the air. Everywhere Merlin looked – nearby and receding into the mist-bands – he could see purple faces, veins bulging, calluses bursting and feet pushing into mounds of thyme so that the air was filled with fragrance. **Now it was his turn to laugh.**

Merlin stood up and put his hands over his face. Those nearest heard him muttering words under his breath. Some wondered if he was praying, but others knew he was not. And then each of the men felt as if the colossal weight of the stones was tiptoeing into their own bodies. Fingertips twitched. Muscles rippled. Jaws clenched. Pupils dilated. And suddenly, as one, each man turned towards the stone with which he had previously contended and placed his arms about it.

After the Giants' Dance had been carried down Killaraus, placed in ships and rebuilt in Amesbury, where the British barons had been killed by Hengist's men, the stones regained their former weight and the soldiers their former weakness. But none who had witnessed the feat ever again put brute strength above all other powers.

When Aurelius returned to Winchester, he contracted a fever. An assassin, sent by the King of Hibernia in revenge for the theft of the Giants' Dance, put on doctor's robes and visited him in his chamber. Receiving medicine from the man, the bronze-haired Aurelius drank. But it was not medicine in the cup, it was a toxic draught. That night, **he fell asleep and did not wake up again.**

They laid Aurelius to rest in the middle of the Giants' Dance, beside the massacred barons. One day, his brother Uther would be placed beside him. In time it would come to be called the Hanging Stones and, after that, **Stonehenge**. And just as Merlin had said, it would indeed stand forever.

History

We believe that Stonehenge was built on Salisbury Plain between 2000 and 3000 BC, with stones from, among other places, the Preseli Hills in Wales. Were you a medieval visitor to Stonehenge, you would probably have had a very different story in mind. To you, the stones would have been quarried by giants in remotest Africa: not real Africa, of course, but a largely fantastical medieval European fantasy of Africa. You might have believed these giants carried the stones across the sea and erected them on a mountain in Ireland, where the rain washed their healing properties into pools for the giants to bathe in. You might then have believed that the stones finally made it to Salisbury Plain hundreds of years later, in the fifth century AD or so, by means of the Merlin's magic, to be a memorial to massacred British nobles. To you, Stonehenge would have been the grave of Britain's slaughtered nobility, as well as the grave of King Aurelius Ambrosius and, later, his brother, King Uther Pendragon. It's to Uther we now turn.

THE STRANGER AT THE GATE

AND THE CONCEPTION OF ARTHUR

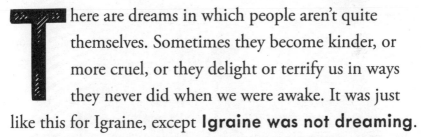

There are dreams in which people aren't quite themselves. Sometimes they become kinder, or more cruel, or they delight or terrify us in ways they never did when we were awake. It was just like this for Igraine, except **Igraine was not dreaming**.

That night, she had been sitting in bed, listening to the ocean, when she heard the doors of the keep being opened. The guards had let someone over the bridge and into the castle. A friend, then. Igraine crept to the entrance of her room. Pressing her ear to the cold wood, she heard a servant's footsteps and men's voices. One voice she recognised as that of her husband, Gorlois.

Igraine threw a robe over her nightclothes and hurried down the stairs. Gorlois was already in the hall.

'What's happened?' she cried, running towards him. He met her with open arms.

'Igraine, my dear, sweet love,' he said into her hair, 'I had to know you were safe.'

She inhaled his familiar smell.

'I am sorry it has come to this, Igraine. As long as you love me, I'm yours.'

He stepped back, and she looked into his face: still those familiar lines, still the curl of his grey eyebrows, but there was **something different about him** . . . something exciting.

Months earlier, when Aurelius Ambrosius had been poisoned, **a star had appeared in the sky, then a dragon had soared from its core** and breathed spears of fire over many lands. Merlin, who was with Uther when the omen occurred, prophesied that Uther, who must now take the throne, would be succeeded by emperors. Uther called himself Pendragon after the sign.

The first thing he did as king was to hold a feast in London for all the nobles in the land. Among them was Gorlois, Duke of Cornwall, who had brought his wife, Igraine. Rumours of her beauty were plentiful, and from the moment she took her seat among the other women, Uther kept his hungry eyes upon her and sent her the finest dishes of food and ewers of the best wine.

In time, Gorlois noticed what the King was doing and his old face crumpled with a frown. He stood and took Igraine's elbow.

'We have to leave,' he said.

But Uther did not want her to go and warned Gorlois that he would take their departure as an insult. Gorlois ignored him, growled his farewells and led Igraine from the room. Returning to Tintagel, an island castle that could only be reached by a narrow spit of rock, Gorlois readied to leave again, telling his wife she should wait there. He wanted to meet Uther in battle at Dameliock, where he had another stronghold.

'Write to me,' he said.

Frustrated and alone, Igraine did not write to Gorlois. The next day, she sat in the window of her room, watching the sea, which was now brilliant beneath the summer sky, and she imagined being married to Uther. **How lovely it would be compared to her life now.** Gorlois was kind, but he was so much older than her, so quiet and so sensible he seemed more of a father than a husband. She yearned for a **companion who laughed more**, as Uther had done at the feast, and who, she was half-ashamed to think it, she wanted to kiss.

Meanwhile, Uther's barons had advised him to forget Igraine and Gorlois and focus on eliminating the Saxon threat. Civil war was a very terrible thing and should not be entered into because of a petty dispute. But Uther ignored them and led his troops to the Cornish duke's castle at Dameliock. As they attacked, he found himself thinking more and more about Igraine. And even though fighting had already begun, he was too impatient to wait a moment longer. He didn't need to *be there* while his troops made his anger known. And while Gorlois was distracted, Igraine would be alone . . .

He called on the magician.

'The solution is this,' said Merlin, who was no longer a child. 'By means of special medicines, I will disguise you as Gorlois, and you can go to Igraine. Then you will have what you want and you can end this war.'

So it was, later that night, that a man who seemed to be Igraine's husband came to see her at Tintagel. And, as you know, she was almost completely deceived, except for the small part of her mind that wondered if it could really be him. He was so different. It was almost as if . . . She pushed the thought away. What mattered was that, at last, **she wanted to kiss him**.

As Igraine put her arms round the disguised Uther,

the real **Gorlois was in danger**. He had ridden out
of Dameliock to fight Uther's warriors and they, more
numerous and agile than he, had pulled him from his
horse. Now, before he had a chance to stand and draw his
sword, they were driving their spears through the gaps in
his armour. Though he had committed no crime, Gorlois
was dead. One of his knights rode straight for Tintagel,
determined to warn Igraine.

It was morning when the exhausted warrior arrived at
the island and was let in by the guards. When he entered
the main chamber, he was amazed by what he saw. His
lord, Gorlois, whose bloody corpse he had just abandoned
at Dameliock, was **in front of him, eating breakfast**.
Of course, what the warrior didn't know was that the man
was really Uther Pendragon, magically disguised by Merlin.
Uther realised he had to leave. Reassuring the knight, as well
as the amazed Igraine, that he, Gorlois, was alive and well,
he left Tintagel. Up on the cliffs, Merlin restored him to
his true shape and the pair rode back to Dameliock. News
spread through the land of Gorlois's death and Igraine did
not understand how he could have been killed on the very
night he had come to her at Tintagel. She knew now that
it couldn't have been her husband who had met her that
night, but she never learned who the man really was. She

wondered **anxiously whether it had been a demon.**

Later, she found out she was pregnant and, fearful for her child's future and despite Uther's part in her first husband's death, **she married the King**. She hoped that such a marriage would give her fatherless child the greatest chance of protection. Merlin felt terrible guilt at what he'd done to help deceive her. But he also knew that the child in her womb **would be a hero**, his name would be Arthur and he would be remembered in legend forever.

History

Historical evidence of Arthur, the greatest king of the Britons, is thin on the ground. The earliest surviving account of Arthur's life appeared around 1136 and dates his birth hundreds of years earlier, when the Saxons were invading the Britons, whom they would one day call the Welsh, for this meant 'foreigners' in their tongue. They were down on their luck. They needed someone to repel the invaders and help them reclaim their ancestral homelands.

In medieval France, a tale emerged of how, at the advice of Merlin, Igraine and Uther handed the baby Arthur over to foster parents without telling anyone else he had been born. The foster parents raised him alongside their older son, Kay. When Uther died without an heir (or so people thought), an anvil – a hard metal block used for shaping heated metals – appeared in the town square where Arthur and Kay lived. It had a **sword driven into**

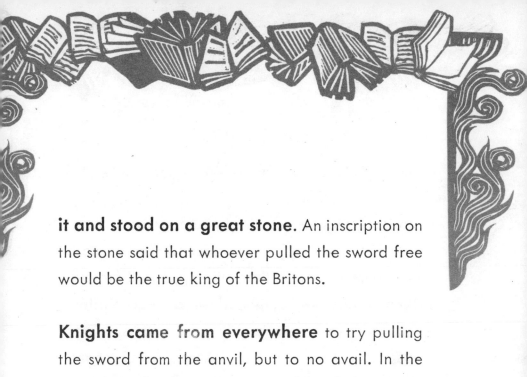

it and stood on a great stone. An inscription on the stone said that whoever pulled the sword free would be the true king of the Britons.

Knights came from everywhere to try pulling the sword from the anvil, but to no avail. In the meantime, there were jousts and battle games to take part in. Kay, now old enough to have been made a knight, had, like everyone else, failed to pull the sword free. Now he wanted to join in with the games. He sent the young Arthur off to fetch him a sword. Crossing through the town square, Arthur saw one stuck in an anvil. He had been so busy helping Kay, he had not heard about its special meaning or read its inscription. Hurrying, not wanting to delay his brother, the boy **jumped up on the stone and lifted the sword free.** When he returned to Kay and his foster father, they could not believe their eyes. His foster father, realising the time had come to tell Arthur his true destiny, admitted the truth about his origins. Arthur was not the lowly squire he thought himself, but the rightful heir to Britain's throne.

Now, let us look under that throne, where we might just see a pair of big brown eyes surrounded by chestnut fur . . .

KING ARTHUR'S BEST FRIEND

HOW A PAW PRINT GOT INTO A STONE

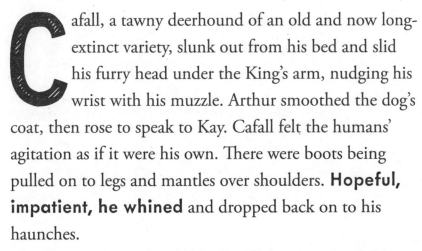

Cafall, a tawny deerhound of an old and now long-extinct variety, slunk out from his bed and slid his furry head under the King's arm, nudging his wrist with his muzzle. Arthur smoothed the dog's coat, then rose to speak to Kay. Cafall felt the humans' agitation as if it were his own. There were boots being pulled on to legs and mantles over shoulders. **Hopeful, impatient, he whined** and dropped back on to his haunches.

Then suddenly the King called his name – 'Cafall!' – and the names of all his friends. His hopes fulfilled, Cafall jumped to his feet, then joined the rest of the hounds as they ran to the call to hunt.

While the riders mounted and prepared, the dogs sniffed the sky. When all was ready, the King brought them a **thin silver hair**. It had been shed from the back of the creature they were hunting, but this was no ordinary animal. They gathered round, as they had done every day for weeks, and inhaled its scent. **It smelled of a man. It smelled of a boar. It was both and it was neither.** It smelled of no creature that Cafall had ever hunted before, but he knew he would track it down. A horn sounded and the hunt took off at once, the hounds sprinting into the trees. As Cafall's blood grew hot, he wove through the briars with his pack, leaping ahead of the galloping horses.

The hunt did not end that day, or even the next. They breathed in the marshy fields, rivers, woodlands, streams and farmsteads, until they came to a hill. An onslaught of hail pelted the branches of the low, scrubby trees, as well as the hunt below, but Cafall hardly felt it. And though he heard the King shout his name, and felt the other dogs dropping back, instinct drove him on. The creature had come this way, he knew it.

Up. Onwards. Closer. Closer. Now, breaking out of the band of woodland, Cafall raced for the summit, where the trail would be strongest. The hail was falling harder now – icy pebbles shooting out of the sky – but Cafall carried on, splashing from stream to boulder to bracken. And then, just as quickly as the hail had come, the clouds began to

clear. When Cafall at last reached the summit, planting
his front paw firm on the highest stone, the landscape was
bright and the wind told his nose where to point.

The creature was dark at first, barely visible on the peak
of a hill across the valley, but suddenly the sun hit and all
at once its form **shone like a lightning ball**, the coat of
silver hairs full of blinding brilliance.

This was Troynt, who had once been a man, but who
had been given the shape of a boar in punishment for a
terrible, long-forgotten crime. Cafall was rooted to the
spot. From deep in his belly, **he began to cry**.

In the malice of the boar's eyes, the dog felt the cruelty
of a hundred leather boots in the ribs, of sticks broken

across the spine, of freezing nights without food or water; of violence, neglect and loneliness. As he stood and trembled, the fire of those eyes passed through him like lightning through a tree, and the very stone under his paw began to melt. He cowered, all his eagerness gone, until, at last, the boar turned its silver head and trotted out of sight.

When he found himself able to move again, Cafall tried to run back to his master, but his paw was stuck. He struggled and whined. Then a hand rested on his back. He recognised the large palm, the scrunching fingers, and turned his nose towards them, smelling the warm sweat, the horse dust and the tang of iron. His master crouched, resting his hand where Cafall's front paw had sunk into the now solid stone. The man felt around each toe, extracting it with gentle care, and Cafall waited and trusted.

After he had released Cafall, the King saw that the stone bore the imprint of a paw. With the dog at his heels, he took the stone and placed it on top of a heap of large stones that the British called a cairn. That day, the hill earned the name Carngafallt, after Cafall. For centuries thereafter, if anyone took the stone away, it would be back on that cairn by morning. King Arthur and his best hound turned and went back down the hill, knuckles brushing fur. All was well again.

History

Stones with imprints of body parts, whether man-made or natural, have an excellent name. They are called petrosomatoglyphs (in Greek, 'petra' means stone, 'soma' means body, and 'glyph' means symbol). All over Britain, not to mention the world, there are stones with carvings or naturally occurring undulations similar to the form of hands, feet or other body parts.

In Wales, there is a hill which goes by the name of Carngafallt. This translates as Cafall's Cairn. It's found in Radnorshire and a work of British history from as early as the ninth century tells us that it used to have a stone bearing Cafall's paw print on top of a pile of stones on its summit. If you took the stone away, it would **always be back where it belonged by the next morning**. When I went to Carngafallt, I had a good look around for the petrosomatoglyph, but I didn't find it. The old magic that made it come back to the top must have gone. But there are other types of magic to sniff out, if you know where to look.

The story you have just read comes from early legends preserved in Welsh and Latin, which describe Arthur going on an epic hunt through Ireland and southwest Britain. But in other tales of Arthur's life, he spends most of his time abroad, where he is said to have conquered thirty kingdoms, including Gaul, Norway and Denmark, reaching even as far as Rome. But then disaster strikes.

Soon after conquering Rome, Arthur receives news that his nephew Mordred has seized the British crown. Arthur rushes home and meets him in battle. There, Arthur is grievously injured and taken away to a place called Avalon.

A prophecy begins to circulate that Arthur will one day return, deliver his people and restore all their former greatness, but until that day, Britain is once again vulnerable to the advancing Saxons. From now, English kingdoms will begin to dominate the southeast and generate their own host of legends . . .

A MOUTHFUL OF FIRE

HOW GRIMSBY GOT ITS NAME

Before his death, Adilbrit had been a lesser king within Britain, ruling Norfolk and part of Denmark under Arthur. His sister married a man called Edelsi, who ruled the territory of Lindsey to the north. When Adilbrit died, his daughter Argentille should have inherited the throne, but Edelsi married her off and took the crown for himself.

Now, she was reclaiming what was rightfully hers. Pushing wet strands of her long, dark hair from her eyes, Argentille drew the knot she was tying tight, fixing the corpse to the stake. **She had done it.** Argentille shook the rain from her nose and checked the ranks around her. She was the only living soul left on the endless marsh and, now that her task was accomplished, the rest would be up to fate.

As she walked back to the encampment, her thoughts

returned to where it had all begun. After stealing her throne, her uncle, Edelsi, had said he would marry her to the 'highest man in the land'. This had not turned out to be a knight or a prince, but Cuaran, a lowly servant of unusual height and large stature. Once they were married, she had been forced to become a servant in her uncle's castle too. This might have been terrible for the young princess, but she soon came to realise she loved Cuaran and he loved her in return.

The pair shared everything, but there was **one mystery about her new husband** that confused Argentille. Every night, Cuaran would turn his back to her as soon as they got into bed and press his face into the pillow. At first, she would stroke his back and ask what he was doing, but he would just breathe as if he were sleeping.

One night, however, a bright light shone through her eyelids, waking her up. Her face was close to Cuaran's cheek and she could smell his warm skin. He must have rolled on to his back. She opened her eyes. At once she saw that the blinding light was coming from his open mouth. **It was a flame, dancing like a crane fly.** Each time he breathed out it grew brighter, spilling over his lips, and each time he breathed in it drew back, licking the insides of his cheeks.

'Cuaran!' she gasped, sitting up. 'You're on fire!'

She shook him by his shoulders. When he awoke, the flame disappeared and they were **both plunged into darkness**. 'You were on fire,' she repeated.

'I know,' he said.

'No, you're not listening. There was fire in your mouth. You need water.'

'I *know*,' he said again, 'It happens when I sleep. I don't know why and I tried not to let you see.'

Argentille fell silent as she worked to understand what he had said. Her mind struggled with the impossibility of it. Was this otherworldly flame really the reason why he had slept with his face pressed into the pillow? Could it really be that this was why he had ignored her every night since they got married? And then, slowly, she started to think it might not be so impossible after all. Argentille, being a princess who had once had access to many books and teachers, knew stories from history and far-off places. Now that she thought about it, she had heard of things like this flame. Usually, they were not cause for embarrassment, but a **sign of special favour.** Usually, they meant something wonderful. She felt for his hand in the dark and took it.

'Why are you ashamed? Better to discover what the

flame means!' said Argentille. Then she whispered, 'You
know what's really shameful?'

'What?'

'Living here as servants in my uncle's castle. There is
some secret behind the fire in your mouth and I think we
should find out what it is. Where does your family live?'

'Grimsby,' Cuaran replied.

'Then we will go there tomorrow.'

Argentille and Cuaran set off the next day, unhindered
by Edelsi, who was glad to see the back of them. When
they arrived in Grimsby, Argentille saw that Cuaran's
hometown was a small fishing port, with houses running
right down to the banks of an estuary called the Humber.
As they walked, Cuaran told her the story of how the King
Humber had drowned
there and given
it his name.
When
he had

finished, they were standing in front of a house. It was the home of his sister, Kelloc.

After welcoming them inside, Kelloc lost no time in stoking the hearth and preparing food for the couple. That evening, when they were fed and rested, Kelloc asked Cuaran a question.

'Do you know who you are, and where your family comes from?'

He answered that he was Cuaran, she was his sister, his father was a fisherman called Grim and his mother, Seburg, had helped him in his trade. But Kelloc shook her head.

'Grim was not born a fisherman,' she said. 'He was born into the nobility of Denmark and when he grew up, he became a knight in the court of King Gunter and Queen Alvive.'

'Our father was a knight?' replied Cuaran, disbelieving, but Kelloc raised a hand for quiet,

'I myself was born there, daughter of Grim and Seburg and goddaughter of the Queen. Sometimes she let me look after her baby, whose name was Havelok. By that time, King Arthur, King of Britain, had conquered Denmark and his armies killed King Gunter. In the midst of the invasion, my mother and father, Grim and Seburg, persuaded Alvive to flee with her infant son. We all boarded a ship for Britain, but while we were out on the cold, dark waves, we were attacked by pirates. Alvive drowned, along with many others, but Grim and Seburg protected me and her baby. Somehow we survived.'

'What a horrible story,' Cuaran said. As Argentille listened, enthralled, and thought she could see where the tale was going. If she was right, then **the flame was indeed a wonderful sign.**

Kelloc continued, 'When the pirates had gone, the ship washed up at the edge of a great estuary. Dragging the pieces of the damaged vessel on to the land, my father and mother used half its timbers to build a shelter and the rest to build a fishing boat. They caught fish in the sea – cod, salmon, turbot, mackerel and many others – and what they didn't eat themselves, they traded for bread. Over the years, more fishermen and women moved to our settlement, built their houses and made a living from the sea. It's because of Grim,' Kelloc said, 'that they called this place Grimsby.'

Cuaran shook his head, 'I had no idea our father and

mother were so great. But I do not understand – when was I born? It must have been after they arrived on the banks of the Humber, for I have no memory of Denmark.'

Kelloc smiled, 'You might well remember Denmark, if you ever visit it. You see, as the town grew, Grim and Seburg told everyone that the Danish Prince Havelok, the baby, was my younger brother. They changed his name to hide his true identity. He grew into a strong little boy and, when he reached manhood, he travelled south to find work as a servant.'

And then Kelloc smiled even more broadly. 'You are Havelok, Cuaran. And your kingship is proven by the flames that dance in your mouth as you sleep, though we used to tease you for it. Now that Arthur is surely dead and a weak British king is ruling in our homeland, I beg you to go home and reclaim your throne. I have some money to help pay your passage.'

When Argentille and Havelok went to bed, she could tell by the darkness that he too was lying awake. But even if he was scared, she was not. **She was eager.** Argentille hoped that with the strength of Cuaran – no, Havelok – combined with her cunning, they would be able to right two wrongs.

As soon as they had saved enough money for the

journey, as well as clothes to replace their threadbare servants' garb, the couple left for Denmark. But they met trouble as soon as they arrived. The King's knights abducted Argentille outside their lodgings and Havelok chased after them, killing one and fleeing with Argentille to a church tower. A knight called Sigar came to see what was afoot. He was one of the older knights who had once known and loved King Gunter. When he saw his old lord's likeness in Havelok's young face, he ordered the soldiers to stand down. Then he invited Argentille and Havelok to be his guests in his castle.

That night, Sigar sent a servant to watch Havelok as he slept. The man confirmed that a flame burned brightly in his mouth, marking him out as **the true and rightful king**. At once, Sigar sent out messengers to summon the other barons who had been loyal to King Gunter.

When they had gathered at Sigar's castle, they offered Havelok a horn that **no one but the rightful king could blow**. Havelok played it with ease. With the proof of the flame and the horn to satisfy them, the barons cheered and pledged themselves to Havelok. Then they set about raising armies against the false British king. With their help, Havelok won back the throne of Denmark.

Argentille was triumphant at her husband's victory,

but she had not forgotten her own hereditary rights, nor
her love for her kingdom of deep skies and slow, shallow
waters. To reclaim them, she would need Havelok and
all the armies now under his command. He was only too
happy to oblige, knowing that he would still be a servant
in Britain were it not for Argentille. Soon, they were sailing
back across the sea.

When they docked, anchoring their ships beyond a
beach of flat sands and salt marshes, word was sent to
Edelsi, claiming the throne and offering peace. He rejected
it at once and battle ensued, but the slaughter was the same
on both sides. When evening had come with no victory,
it was agreed they would meet again the next day. The
survivors returned to the camp and Argentille heard their
news. There were so many dead and injured for her sake.
In the privacy of her tent, she cried. She could not watch
more lives being lost, nor live with the suffering of the
injured. There had to be something she could do. She shut
her eyes and made a plan.

That night, in the hollow, rain-spattered darkness, she
led fifty men back on to the battlefield. As they went, they
harvested hazel poles from the woodlands. Reaching the
place where the battle had been fought, they drove the
stakes in lines into the field. Then, as the rain hammered

on to their cloaks, they tied the bodies of dead soldiers to the poles, so that each was standing upright. She and the men worked with sober horror. When they had done as she had asked, she sent them shivering back to their fires and tents. Then Argentille checked their work, securing the final knots on her own. She stood back and saw rows of **dark corpses standing as though alive**, their eyes reflecting the storm. She prayed the plan would work.

In the morning, Argentille rose early and walked to the edge of the battlefield. The rain had stopped and, as the sun burned off the morning mist and dried the stands of reeds, she watched Havelok and his soldiers arrange themselves between the ranks of the dead. It was convincing – **the army looked twice its real size**. Next, she saw her uncle's scouts survey the assembled troops and leave to report to the King. When they returned, they delivered a message to Havelok. He raised his arms in victory and she knew what his gesture meant: her uncle had been fooled and had surrendered his crown to Argentille. She kissed the damp ground in relief.

And that's how Grimsby got its name and how many Danes came to live in the north-eastern part of Britain. For the rest of their lives, Argentille and Havelok would rule their kingdoms together, and their people would travel to and fro across the cold North Sea, as if it were no more than a stream.

History

In medieval times, towns often had an exciting origin legend that might have been performed as a play or read aloud on high days and holidays. The origin story of Grimsby, now an industrial fishing port on the north-east coast of England, was the story of Havelok and Argentille. The newly-weds can even be seen on the medieval town seal, a metal coin-like object that would have been pushed into melted wax to authorise important documents.

The story of Argentille and Havelok is set just after the defeat of Arthur, around the fifth century AD, and offers a mythical explanation for the historical link between Denmark and the north-east coast of Britain. This link is real, even if the story itself is myth.

In the Middle Ages, Norse (that is, Scandinavian) presence in Britain was largely the result of the Vikings. In some cases, the Vikings were bands

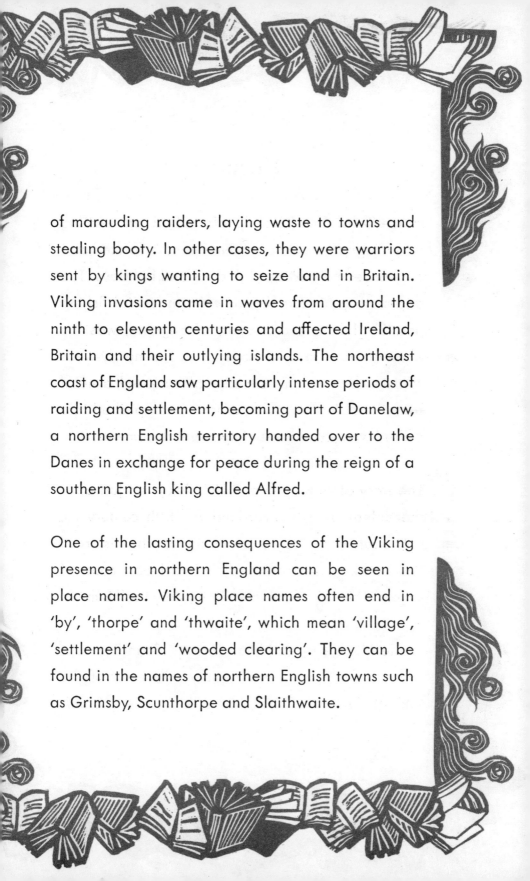

of marauding raiders, laying waste to towns and stealing booty. In other cases, they were warriors sent by kings wanting to seize land in Britain. Viking invasions came in waves from around the ninth to eleventh centuries and affected Ireland, Britain and their outlying islands. The northeast coast of England saw particularly intense periods of raiding and settlement, becoming part of Danelaw, a northern English territory handed over to the Danes in exchange for peace during the reign of a southern English king called Alfred.

One of the lasting consequences of the Viking presence in northern England can be seen in place names. Viking place names often end in 'by', 'thorpe' and 'thwaite', which mean 'village', 'settlement' and 'wooded clearing'. They can be found in the names of northern English towns such as Grimsby, Scunthorpe and Slaithwaite.

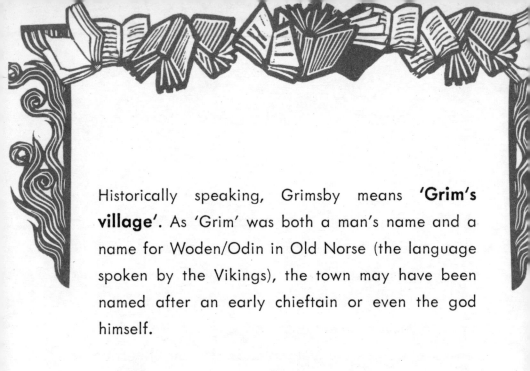

Historically speaking, Grimsby means **'Grim's village'**. As 'Grim' was both a man's name and a name for Woden/Odin in Old Norse (the language spoken by the Vikings), the town may have been named after an early chieftain or even the god himself.

Origin myths for towns are called civic myths. They helped give townspeople a sense of shared heritage and pride in their home. Does such a myth exist for your village, town or city? If not, it surely needs one.

THE FIRST THREEFOLD DEATH

AND MERLIN'S FORGOTTEN SISTER

There are many cracks in the floorboards of history. Sometimes one is wide enough for a story or character to slip through and become lost among centuries of debris. This tale is about one of those characters. **If you put your eye to the crack, you will see her as she once was: sleeping**, not in the piled dust of the ages, but on a simple bed in a bare room, curled up next to her brother. In those days, she was barely three years old and he was no more than ten. Her warm, bare feet rested on his knees under the covers, and her eyelids flickered as she dreamed. Her name was Gwendydd and her brother's name was Merlin.

Of course, **Merlin was fathered by a demon** and maybe it was the same with her. That would, perhaps, explain her dreams, which were vivid and strange.

However, for now she would go unnoticed. When Vortigern's soldiers came looking for a child with no human father, they had been told to search for a boy. They found a boy and they took him away. That night, Gwendydd would not have her brother's warm knees on which to rest her feet and no one to whom she could whisper her dreams in the moments between waking and rising for morning prayer.

When Gwendydd grew up, she appeared more confident than her brother and more at home among people. She married Rhydderch, the king of the northern Britons and they stayed together, not exactly in love, but not unhappy either, for many decades.

Rhydderch's and Gwendydd's chamber windows looked out across the vast black forests of Calidon. Beyond them were the territories of the hostile Picts and Scots. Calidon, by then, was where her brother Merlin had gone to live.

After the disappearance of Arthur, when Merlin had grown tired of watching the endless cycle of new kings and new barons, he retreated to the forest's towering pines. Occasionally, he still visited Gwendydd and Rhydderch, though the visits rarely went well. Whenever he returned to the wild, he spent many days in stillness beside the moss-encircled pools and gorse-covered outcrops of the forest.

Stirred up by his time among people, he found peace in the wild.

Worried for his health, especially in winter, Gwendydd would sometimes send a scout to look for Merlin. But such was the vastness of the forest and the timidity of her brother that **finding him was about as easy as tracking a polecat**. More often than not, her scout would return with nothing.

One day, however, the scout saw a human shape moving at the top of a mountain, the peak of which rose out of the dark ocean of trees. It was autumn and the forest was going to sleep. Hitching his pack, the scout plunged into the branches, tramping over the thick carpet of earth, pine needles, fungi and ferns, to get to the mountain and climb. When he reached the summit, tired and smudged from where he had scraped against the tree trunks, he saw Merlin sitting there beside a spring of fresh water. It reflected the white light of the sky.

Merlin was **singing to the water about the loss of all the beautiful things of spring and summer.**

'Oh cuckoo, where is your song? Oh swift, I long to hear you again. From the bright greenery, the voices of birds used to swell and lift the spirits. Their melody used to help me sleep.'

The scout listened, then began to open his pack. From it, he withdrew a **wooden musical instrument shaped like the end of a paddle**. It had a circular cut-out at one end, over which were drawn several strings of dried and tightly stretched animal guts. It was called a lyre and the scout was an expert musician. Thinking of the call of the cuckoo – a high note, then a lower note, sung as a pair – he began to pluck the strings and play a melody full of the liveliness of spring.

Over by the pool, Merlin heard the music. It was lovely. **It was just as soothing as the water**. Then the musician began to sing about Merlin's former wife, Gwendolena, and his sister, Gwendydd. In soaring, spiralling notes, he sang truthfully about how much they loved him and wished he would come home. Merlin thought of them both and how much he missed them too. Then he stood up and came to stand beside the scout. **Together, singing, they walked down the mountain** and all the way back to the court.

When they arrived, the town around the palace was full of people going about their daily business. The cacophony of their voices struck Merlin's ears like the clash of metal against metal and returned him to a battlefield on which he had long ago descended into madness. He turned to leave but Rhydderch had sent soldiers to wait for Merlin and seize him if he tried to escape. They put manacles on his hands and took him to the palace.

The King was tired of hearing his wife worrying about her strange brother and thought that if he kept Merlin by force, he could silence her. No longer peaceful, but offended and sad, Merlin was led into a fine hall and brought before the King.

When Gwendydd came in, she did not, at first, see her brother. She took her seat and Rhydderch reached out, teasing a leaf from between the strands of her long grey hair, which was arranged in an elaborate braid. At first she smiled and thanked him, but then she noticed Merlin. **Seeing the chains around his arms**, she was about to demand an explanation from Rhydderch when her brother let out a loud laugh. It bounced off the beams above their heads. It was a knowing laugh, a laugh that seemed to say that, by plucking the leaf out of his wife's hair, Rhydderch had been a fool. By the look on his face, Rhydderch did not like it one bit.

'Why are you laughing?' asked Rhydderch. Merlin said nothing. Again, Rhydderch said, 'Why did you laugh?'

But the old man made no reply. Then Rhydderch tried to coax him into explaining himself by offering him gifts, to which Merlin said, 'The acorns of Calidon are enough for me.'

'Take off his chains,' ordered Rhydderch. When he was unshackled, Merlin said, so that all the people could hear, 'I laughed because you were so trusting when you took the leaf out of my sister's hair. She's your wife and you think she's innocent. But I know, thanks to my gift, that it got there among the bushes of the palace gardens, where she has just been with her lover.'

Rhydderch turned angry eyes on Gwendydd, who understood that it was not her disloyalty that enraged him, but the fact that **Merlin had declared it in front of all the court.** She was regretting sending the scout to the forest now that Merlin had been chained. But if she played this right, she could escape her husband's anger, have her brother released and, in time, prove his prophetic skill. All her wits alert, Gwendydd spoke before her husband could open his mouth. 'And you believe my brother, do you? The one you call a madman?'

Then she turned to Merlin, 'Dear brother, tell me how this boy will die.'

She beckoned to a boy standing among the guards. Looking nervous, he stepped forward. Pointing to him, she tilted her head at Merlin. He returned her gaze.

'Why, sister, he will die by falling off a cliff.'

The boy looked shocked.

'Is that so?' she said.

At this, everyone set about muttering, but before Gwendydd could ask the next question, the servants entered with platters of food for dinner. Tables and benches were brought into the middle of the hall and for a while everyone was distracted, getting started on the evening meal.

Gwendydd now walked among the moving bodies of the crowd. It wasn't long till she found the boy whom Merlin had said would fall from a cliff. She whispered to him to leave the hall, cut his long hair and change his clothes. **He obeyed without hesitation.** When he got back, everyone was sitting down and eating. The Queen called to Merlin from her seat.

'Brother, dearest, what about *this* boy. How will *this* boy die?'

Merlin gave her a shrewd glance.

'He will die hanging from a tree.'

She nodded at her brother. 'So you say,' she replied.

The boy looked a little relieved. He could not die by falling off a cliff *and* hanging from a tree. Around him, a few **people laughed**. They recognised him and thought Merlin had been fooled by his change of clothes. *Not so wise as the old stories say*, they whispered between themselves.

When dinner was over, the courtiers rose and began mingling. The Queen found the boy again. She said to him, 'Go to my room and have one of my ladies dress you in her clothes.'

The boy obeyed. When he returned, his head veiled and his body swathed in a silk dress, heads turned to see such a tall young maiden making her way into the hall. Despite his disguise, many of them recognised the figure as the boy already destined to die twice. **They nudged each other, giggling**, and settled down for the next part of the entertainment.

'Dearest brother,' called Gwendydd over the hushed crowd. 'What about this girl? How will she die?'

'She'll drown in a river,' Merlin replied.

Gwendydd smiled with relief. She was safe, for now, and her husband would no longer care about Merlin's accusation. As for Merlin, he would be set free and, one day, this moment would be remembered as proof of his power. For now, however, everyone was laughing at him. Merlin had predicted **three separate deaths for one person and that, of course, was impossible.**

Merlin stood with his eyes fixed on the wooden ceiling beams, his ears full of the laughter of the court. They didn't see, as he did, that when the boy whose deaths he had predicted was a fully grown man, he would be out hunting a stag, charging over many terrains. Without checking his speed, he would reach the edge of a cliff. By the time he noticed it, it would be too late to stop his horse. Both would tumble, falling, speeding towards the churning river beneath. But before he hit the water, the man would strike a tree growing out the side of the rock face. He would clatter through the branches until he had almost fallen through completely, except, at the last moment, his foot would become hooked on a bough. As he hung upside down from the tree, dazed by the fall, his head and shoulders would dangle in the water and he would drown.

So it would be. The boy would one day die by falling from a cliff, hanging from a tree and drowning in a river. When, years later, all this had come to pass, news came back to the court of the man's threefold death. Then, many remembered Merlin's prediction and **understood he had been telling the truth**.

Gwendydd cried at the city gates as Merlin returned to the forest. Her sadness was so great that she fell to the ground and tore at her clothes, her carefully woven grey hair falling from its clasps. It wasn't just that she would miss him. It was that part of her yearned to follow.

History

In the Middle Ages, the Caledonian forests would have formed a barrier over the highlands of what is now Scotland. Lurking under the evergreen boughs of Scots pine were predators, now long-extinct: bears, lynxes and wolves. For medieval humans, Calidon was a dark and perilous place.

In his old age, stories say that **Merlin becomes a Wildman** who frequently leaves society to spend time in the forest. In some tales, he has a sister called Gwendydd. She cares for him and often laments his refusal to live in the court, fearing for his safety among the trees, especially in the depths of winter. However, as the story develops, we begin to wonder whether her real wish is to run away as well.

Since the Middle Ages, humans have turned out to be even more dangerous than bears; the Caledonian forests and their wildlife have suffered terribly at our hands. We should be very grateful for expert

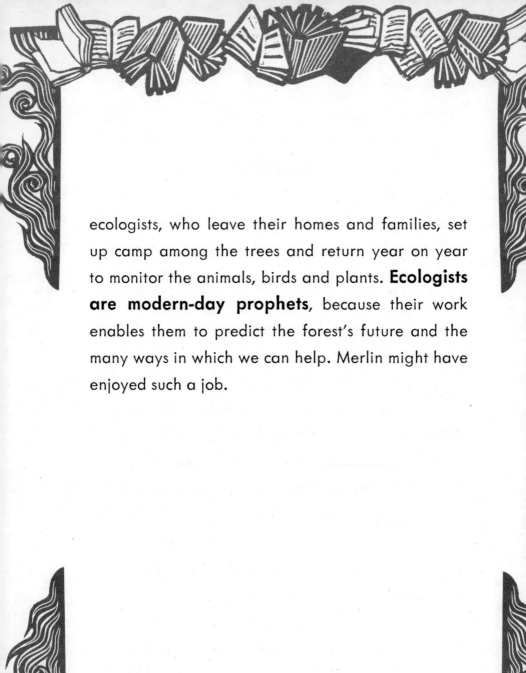

ecologists, who leave their homes and families, set up camp among the trees and return year on year to monitor the animals, birds and plants. **Ecologists are modern-day prophets**, because their work enables them to predict the forest's future and the many ways in which we can help. Merlin might have enjoyed such a job.

GWENDYDD'S DREAM

AND THE DAY SHE BECAME A PROPHET

Several cold winters passed and Merlin grew ever more remote from the court. He lived like a wild animal, but his nature was still human and he still missed those few people he loved. Among them were Gwendydd and his former wife, Gwendolena.

Many **animals made their homes in the vast forest** of Calidon. There were boar, stags, sows and does, the kind of animals that the nobility hunted for their feasts. One morning, as Merlin woke up among the mist-shrouded and sweet-smelling trees, he perceived, thanks to the spirit that lived within him, that Gwendolena was getting married again. He made up his mind to go and see her and pay his respects however he could. He had little to offer as a gift except for the animals with which he shared the trees, but they would be a handsome present even by the standards of the court. Standing up from his bed among the ferns, he strode off into the trees.

As he walked, Merlin **encouraged the beasts he saw to follow him.** There were wild boar with their striped piglets, which trotted together, their dainty feet and bristly bodies jostling the fallen leaves. Then there were deer – young bucks, fawns and does, as well as the handsome stags. It being autumn, some had lost their antlers. Goats came too, which lived wild in the forest. Soon, Merlin was surrounded by animals.

He **climbed on to the back of the largest stag,** which had antlers as wide as Merlin was tall and a body so deeply furred that Merlin had no need for reins. His fingers creaked into its warm, rust-coloured shoulders and held on tight. Beneath his legs, Merlin could feel the beast's muscles. **Then Merlin began to lead the herd on their long journey** out of the trees, towards the court of King Rhydderch and the wedding of Gwendolena. The animals would be his gift.

When they reached the open plains, Merlin let the stag run, enjoying the cold in his hair and beard and the flow of the muscles beneath his calves. This was the only warhorse he wanted and the wild the only palace.

It was late morning before King Rhydderch's strongholds came into view. The settlement there would one day be called Glasgow. Merlin rode towards it, the animals either side of him in two long lines, and arrived at the main gate.

'Gwendolena,' he called from his mount. 'I have brought you gifts to honour your marriage!'

The bride, who was getting ready in her room, heard Merlin's voice and rushed down to see him. He knew that **she had never stopped loving him**, even if she had accepted that he would never be happy living the life of a married man, never comfortable in the court. He began to return her smile, when, from somewhere overhead, came the sound of laughter.

In one of the upper-storey windows, the bridegroom was pointing at Merlin and laughing. **His teeth glowed white in the darkness.**

The laughter struck Merlin's mind like a hammer blow and at once he was back outside Carmarthen, children teasing him for his demon father. And then he was among the men on mount Killaraus, scorned for being too small to move the Giants' Dance. And then he was standing in front of King Rhydderch, being mocked for predicting three deaths for one person. And then he saw himself as he was now, but through the bridegroom's unkind eyes: naked, old, his chest a hollow cave, his heart like a flapping moth. And as groom laughed at the sight of the old man and his gift of muddy beasts, a **vengeful fury rose in Merlin like a dragon.**

Merlin seized the base of each of the stag's antlers and pulled them from its head. The beast bellowed, the weight of a year's growth lifted a little too soon. Then the old magician hurled the antlers, tine over tine, through the air and into the open window.

Merlin heard the spatter of blood hitting the back wall of the chamber, but he did not wait to see if the groom would return to the window. **He wheeled the stag around and charged back towards the forest.** As he rode, he felt as if a tree had been uprooted in his heart. Meanwhile, high up in the chamber, the body of the groom was lying on the ground, a dark stain seeping into the floor under his head.

News of the terrible event spread through the court and at last Gwendydd understood that her brother would

never be safe nor happy among people. Old though she might now be, the time had come for her to decide where her loyalties lay.

Packing bags with only as much as she would need, Gwendydd left Rhydderch and went to join Merlin in Calidon. In that time, another great prophet called Taliesin joined them. They lived in a **simple leaf-woven hall deep among the trees** and though they helped each other, they rarely spoke, and each knew they were free to come and go as they pleased.

Sometimes, on especially bitter nights, Gwendydd and Merlin would sleep on the same mattress of dry bracken, covered by a woollen blanket. She would rest the soles of her feet on his knees and remember how it had been when they were children. Now, as then, she had vivid dreams. When they were children, she had asked Merlin what they meant and he had not always responded. These days she knew better. She had to prepare her question in a very special way.

In the mornings after one of her dreams, Gwendydd would spread a slice of bread with butter and fresh herbs.

Then she would bring out a silver goblet of wine, a hornful of mead, a wooden pitcher of beer, a white bowl of milk and a clay jug of water. The bread and the vessels she would place before her brother. Merlin would make strange responses to each of these things. Looking at the sandwich he would say, 'You don't eat bread from the middle, so the Saxons will not make war everywhere.'

Then he would peer into the silver goblet of wine and say, 'This drink is not for me, because wine makes the rich poor.'

The mead, made of fermented honey and water, he refused because it brought sickness to the well. The beer he rejected because it made the wise senseless. But the milk he drained from its pure white bowl.

'Milk,' he would say, wiping his mouth, **'nourishes the frail and empowers the strong.'**

Finally, pushing the clay jug of water towards him, Gwendydd would tell him, 'Water is one of the four elements, sent by God.'

To this, Merlin would reply, 'Sister, you never spoke a truer word. This is the best of them all. Water will satisfy my thirst till Judgement Day.'

Only when Merlin was full of nourishing food and drink would Gwendydd ask him to interpret her dreams.

'My dearest brother,' she said, 'last night I dreamed that I was standing in a graveyard full of very young women. All of them were pregnant and near to giving birth. But then I noticed that the children in their bellies were talking to each other. It filled me with wonder and I want to know what it means.'

Merlin smiled and said, 'The young women mean that there will be a time in the future when **marriages will be arranged between those who are hardly old enough**. As for the conversations between the children in their wombs, that means that their **offspring will be unusually wise**. At that time a fifteen year old will be wiser than a man of sixty is today!'

Gwendydd did not always know what to make of Merlin's interpretations, but she wrote them down with tools she had brought from the court.

One day, Gwendydd was standing in the leafy hall, watching swallows flit in and out of the nests under the eaves. All of a sudden, sunlight pierced the clouds and filled the whole chamber with glorious golden beams. She found herself dazzled, amazed by the beauty of the sight. Feeling as though the light played a kind of music, she began to sway. As she swayed, words came into her mouth and she spoke them. From her lips came a long stream of wondrous predictions. Standing there bathed in light, Gwendydd spoke of enchained bishops in Oxford, twin moons soaring over Winchester, dangerous sea crossings, famine and war. It was her first prophecy, and the gift for which she would be remembered.

When she had finished, she turned to see Merlin standing in the doorway. His eyes crinkling with love, he said, 'My book is shut, dear sister. The work that has been mine now falls to you.'

History

Medieval stories often describe Merlin's ability to tell the future as coming from **a spirit that lives inside him.** The story about Gwendydd's dreams and the other one about her receiving Merlin's gift are found in two separate sources, one written in Welsh, one in Latin. The second one describes a formal transfer of responsibility from brother to sister. Merlin's assurance suggests Gwendydd will now be able to do more than dream about the future. She will understand what those dreams mean as well. Although Merlin is coming to the end of his life, his prophetic spirit lives on.

And so Gwendydd lived with her new gift, deep in the Caledonian Forest. Perhaps she passed it on to someone else, who passed it on to someone else, who in turn passed it on, and so on, through the ages. If so, then perhaps it now dwells in the mind of a present-day ecologist, sitting in the entrance of her tent, sipping tea from a flask, interpreting the signs.

MUNGO MEETS A WILDMAN

THE DEATH OF MERLIN

While the aged Merlin was still wandering Calidon, a bishop built a church beside Rhydderch's court. His name was Kentigern, though he was better known as Mungo.

One evening, as Mungo prayed among the trees of Calidon, he heard the sound of running feet. Looking up, he saw an old man with hair and a beard like tangling ivy. Mungo knew him at once to be Merlin, the soothsayer of Arthur's court, who had fled to the woods in his old age and of whom so many stories were told. Mungo caught up with the old man and took hold of his arm.

'Why do you live out here on your own?' Mungo asked.

'I have done terrible things.'

Then Merlin began to weep, slipping from Mungo's grasp and running into the trees. The bishop did not follow him, but said a prayer for Merlin's soul.

Some time after this, Merlin took to sitting on a crag near the church, shrieking prophecies into the valley. Within their chapter house, the monks whispered between themselves.

'It is Merlin!'

'He built Stonehenge with magic!'

'He was fathered by a demon!'

Mungo began to **wish he had never met the old man in the trees with his doom-laden prophecies.** Now Merlin had started asking to be blessed in the church by receiving the Eucharist, also known as Holy Communion. Mungo was irritated and said to the monks, 'He has spoken nothing but lies since taking his place on that rock. God sent him to the wild. That is where he belongs.'

But the **monks begged him to have mercy.**

'If you think he's so wise,' Mungo continued, 'why don't you go and ask him how he will die?'

So they asked him, and he said, 'Today I shall die by being stoned and clubbed to death.'

The clerics rushed back to Mungo. He was going to be murdered! What should they do?

'Ask him the same question again.'

They did and Merlin declared, 'Today my body will be pierced by a stake.'

The brothers relayed his reply.

'I do not think we should give him the Eucharist', said Mungo.

But the monks went to Merlin a third time and asked him of his death once more, eager to save his soul. This time Merlin told them, 'Today I will drown.'

At this, the clerics asked why he insisted on lying if he wanted them to grant his request. But Merlin just pulled at his clematis hair and cried, 'I have spoken the truth!'

The monks went into the church and begged Bishop Mungo to give him the Eucharist. And at last, seeing the old man weeping on the rock, he brought Merlin into the monastery, helped him wash and dressed him in fresh robes. Then the whole company gathered in the church. And just as the evening sun entered by the west window, Merlin approached Mungo and took the sacred bread in his mouth. And when he had eaten it, **he made the last prophecy of his life**: 'If I die today, the King will follow me within a year.' From the moment Merlin had entered the church, he had been still and quiet, but as soon as the blessing was finished, he flung off his robes and **ran naked back to the woods.**

The next
morning, shepherds
from a village called
Drumelzier confessed they
had mistaken a Wildman
for a thief and attacked him

with clubs and stones, causing him to fall over a precipice.
When they realised their mistake and ran after him, they
found him face down in a fish pond. He had landed on
sharp stake, which had been poking out of the
ground. Hearing all this, Mungo realised
that **Merlin had predicted his death
correctly**: he had been clubbed to death,
he had been pierced by a stake and he had
drowned. And just as Merlin had
been correct in this, so his last
prophecy came true. Within a
year, the court of the Briton King
Rhydderch was sacked by Áedán,
King of the Scotti, who had crossed the
sea from Hibernia to build strongholds in
northern Britain. That was the beginning of
the kingdom of the Scots.

History

Merlin's old age and journey towards death mark the end of the Britons' supremacy over Britain, but the medieval stories do not always agree on how he died. In some stories, he is **tricked by his student into entering an enchanted sleep**, from which he will never wake up. I have offered you one which features the character of Mungo. Mungo is the patron saint of modern-day Glasgow and the cathedral there is dedicated to him. Lots of stories exist about Mungo too, including one in which he brings a dead robin back to life. You may have noticed that Merlin dies a similar kind of threefold death to the one he predicts for the boy in Rhydderch's court. This is an example of a 'trope', which is **a storytelling device that can be used in lots of different ways.** Another trope you've met in this book is that of a character exiled, cut off from all ties of family and society, so that

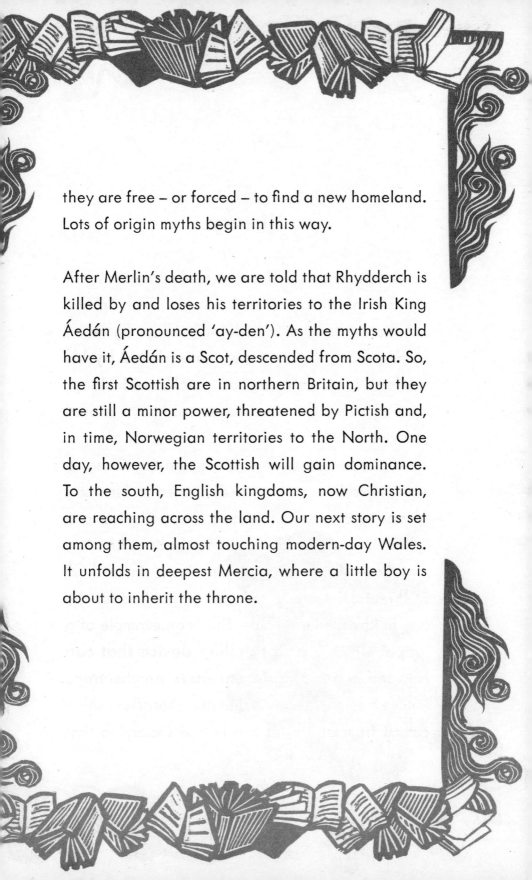

they are free – or forced – to find a new homeland. Lots of origin myths begin in this way.

After Merlin's death, we are told that Rhydderch is killed by and loses his territories to the Irish King Áedán (pronounced 'ay-den'). As the myths would have it, Áedán is a Scot, descended from Scota. So, the first Scottish are in northern Britain, but they are still a minor power, threatened by Pictish and, in time, Norwegian territories to the North. One day, however, the Scottish will gain dominance. To the south, English kingdoms, now Christian, are reaching across the land. Our next story is set among them, almost touching modern-day Wales. It unfolds in deepest Mercia, where a little boy is about to inherit the throne.

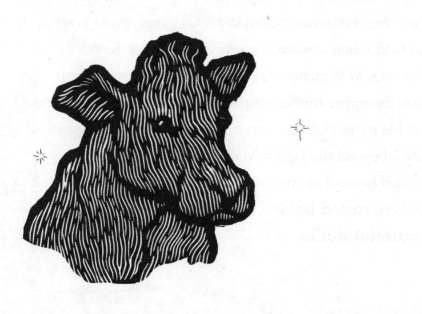

THE LAMP TREE, THE WHITE DOVE AND THE WISE COW

THE STORY OF SAINT KENELM

Curly-haired Kenelm was the only son of an English king whose domains stretched from Gloucestershire to Staffordshire, forming a kingdom then known as Mercia. He lived until around 900 AD, in days when the Saxons had begun calling themselves the English and held much of what we now call England. Kenelm's home was in Winchcombe, among the Cotswold Hills. From the upper timbers of the palace where he lived, it was possible to see right the way across the trees of the Severn Valley, beyond the jagged Malverns, to the Welsh lands, guarded beyond by mountains. Kenelm's nurse, Olwen, had been **raised behind those mountains and told wonderful stories.**

Olwen was round in stature and warm in heart. She had hairs on her chin and tales in her blood. She told young Kenelm of a time when her people had roamed the whole island, led by giant warlords who built enormous cities, the ruins of which were still standing. She knew **how to interpret these tales too**. That story is about extinction, she would say, and this one about the call to a higher service.

Olwen and Kenelm were both Christians and she had told him many stories of saints, filling him with a desire to become one himself. **He wanted to be a survivor, an adventurer and a hero.** When he played, he would pretend to speak to the birds, pray in tongues or live on the back of a whale. He would banish dragons and vanquish devils. Sometimes he would fast till he was faint with hunger. By these means, he really did become very holy, though he did not know it himself.

Kenelm was just seven years old when his father died and the throne of Mercia passed to him. His older sister, Quendryda, felt cheated. She was older than Kenelm and resented being overlooked. She decided she would do whatever it took to seize the crown. First, she tried poisoning her little brother, but she must have concocted the drink wrongly, because it had no effect. Then she went to Kenelm's tutor, Askobert, who was in love with her. She told him to take Kenelm on a day's ride, all the way to the northern edge of the kingdom, where he would find the forest of Clent. There, she said, he should kill the boy, then come back and claim his reward. Askobert **promised to do the deed**.

That night, after Kenelm had said his prayers and fallen asleep, he dreamed that a tree was growing at the foot of his bed and filling the sky. He started to climb, using the giant cracks in the bark as hand- and footholds. When he looked up, he saw the canopy was ablaze with lanterns and laden with flowers. Though the tree was very tall, Kenelm had soon reached the uppermost branches and was crawling along them to find a seat among the flowers. **Never before had he seen anything so grand and perfect** as the tree in which he was sitting. And when he looked ahead, he saw a great landscape unfolding before him. He recognised the hills and rivers of his own kingdom: Gloucestershire, Worcestershire and Warwickshire and beyond, all within his view.

But then he heard footsteps coming from the ground below. **Someone with an axe had begun chopping at the tree trunk,** making great chips fly and the whole canopy shake.

'No!' cried Kenelm from his perch on the high bough, but the person did not stop. He struck away at the vast trunk until he was surrounded by a mound of chips and splinters. And then Kenelm felt the tree beneath him begin to fall. And then **he was tumbling with it**, in a whirl of lanterns, blooms, fruit and branches.

He braced himself, expecting to hit the ground, but suddenly, rather than falling, Kenelm was flying, rising up through the air as the tree crashed around him. He had wings. **He was a dove, free of the crushing branches and the hard forest floor.** He left the earth behind, taking in the view of the Malverns, the snaking river, the vast palace woods, and he felt a breathless, easy joy.

When he awoke, he was back in his bed, looking up into the concerned face of Olwen. Hearing cries from his room, she had come running. Kenelm described the dream to her and she told him, crying, what it meant.

Askobert came to find Kenelm the next morning and offered to take him hunting. Knowing what was to come, the boy smiled and took his tutor's hand.

'I'd like that,' he said.

Kenelm chatted happily as they rode, and though the weather was mild and the roads well-tended, it still took them a whole day to get where there were going. As the sun began to set, they entered a forest that covered two lonely hills.

When Askobert had led Kenelm some way into the

trees, the boy said, 'I would like to sleep. Here will do.'

He had already hopped off his horse, laid his cloak on the ground and put down the stick he had been using as a staff. Then he curled up on the cloak and, within a few moments, his breathing was deep and slow. Askobert took the chance to find **the best place for a grave**. He wandered until he found a glade deeper in the woods. Then he set to work.

Tying up the horses, he took a small spade from his satchel and started digging. Then he jumped. He'd heard the voice of Kenelm, who was standing right beside him.

'You're wasting your effort. I'll die in another place tonight. The staff in my hand will show you.'

Askobert **felt fear rising in him** as he followed the child to a clearing between the hills. There Kenelm pushed the staff into the ground. It grew upwards and branched outwards. **Buds formed, leaves unfurled, roots drove into the soil.** Then the child began to chant a psalm in a high young voice, walking on a little further. 'Te Deum laudamus,' he sang, as he knelt down beneath a hawthorn tree. *We praise you, God.*

The tutor squeezed his eyes shut as he brought down his knife and performed the deed that Quendryda had sent him to do. Then there was a flap of wings and the cooing

of a dove. Askobert buried Kenelm where he lay, which
was easy enough in the soft earth, though the sight of the
blood mingling with the rust-coloured soil repulsed him.
He consoled himself with the **knowledge that he had
done as he was told**. He rode back to Winchcombe to
claim his reward.

Quendryda was delighted by the news that Kenelm
was dead, but sent Askobert away with nothing. She made
herself queen and forbade mention of her brother. And he
might have been forgotten altogether, had it not been for
the cow.

The cow, which belonged to an old woman in Clent,
had taken to spending each day in the wooded valley,
sitting on a particular spot beneath a hawthorn tree,
refusing to eat, but yielding bucketfuls of sweet milk every
morning and night. The villagers began to call that part
of the valley Cowbach, which today has come to be called
Clatterbach.

News of the cow reached the Pope in Rome. While
he was saying mass, a snow-white dove flew down to the
altar and laid a piece of parchment before him. The golden
words upon it were in English, which the Pope could
not speak, so natives of that land were brought forth and
they read the letter aloud: 'Beneath a thorn tree in Clent,

Cowbach, the King's son Kenelm lies.'

Astonished, the Pope sent word to Wilfrid, Archbishop
of Canterbury, who assembled a search party. Travelling to
Clent, they found the cow and, beneath her, the grave of
the innocent child. When the company lifted him from
the earth, a spring bubbled up at the spot, marking it as
sacred. Word was then sent to the monks of Winchcombe,
who vowed to build Kenelm a shrine. And so **the body
began its journey back home**, and when it was only

half a mile from the town, another spring of fresh water burst babbling from the turf.

Quendryda was in the chapel, quite ignorant of the dove, the cow and the search party. But when she saw the great procession of women and men on the hills above Winchcombe, **she felt a sudden dread**. Asking her servant what the procession could mean, the girl said, 'Haven't you heard? Your brother's body has been found!'

Quendryda snatched up her psalter, which contained all the holy psalms. Turning to the one which has long served as a curse upon oppressors, she hissed the words, her eyes darting to the window after every line. She hoped the words would bring vengeance down on the people who had found her brother, but she should have taken more care.

No sooner had she uttered the final malediction than her **eyeballs popped out and landed on the page**. When the company with Kenelm's body entered the church, they found Quendryda dead.

Later, the book was displayed beside St Kenelm's miracle-working shrine, where all could see and rejoice in the two round stains left on the parchment by her eyeballs. And just as gloriously as Kenelm was honoured, that's how little they honoured the Queen. They threw her into a ditch that people used as a toilet.

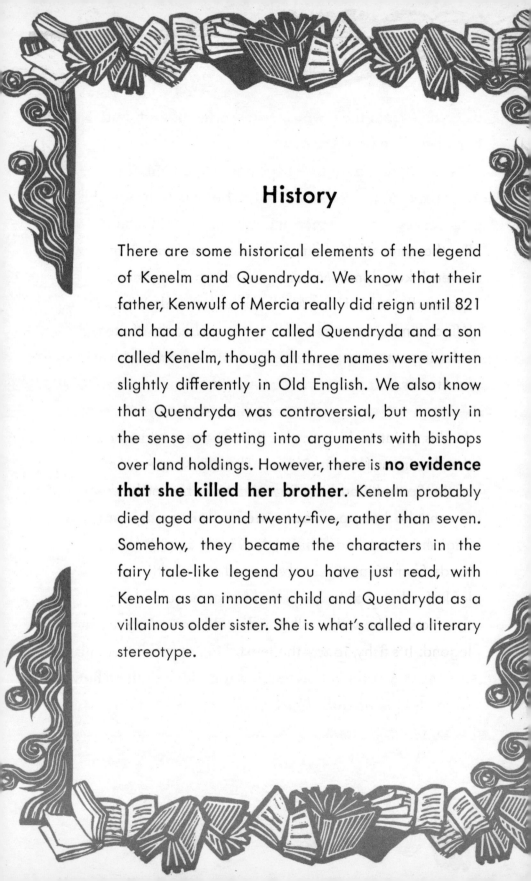

History

There are some historical elements of the legend of Kenelm and Quendryda. We know that their father, Kenwulf of Mercia really did reign until 821 and had a daughter called Quendryda and a son called Kenelm, though all three names were written slightly differently in Old English. We also know that Quendryda was controversial, but mostly in the sense of getting into arguments with bishops over land holdings. However, there is **no evidence that she killed her brother.** Kenelm probably died aged around twenty-five, rather than seven. Somehow, they became the characters in the fairy tale-like legend you have just read, with Kenelm as an innocent child and Quendryda as a villainous older sister. She is what's called a literary stereotype.

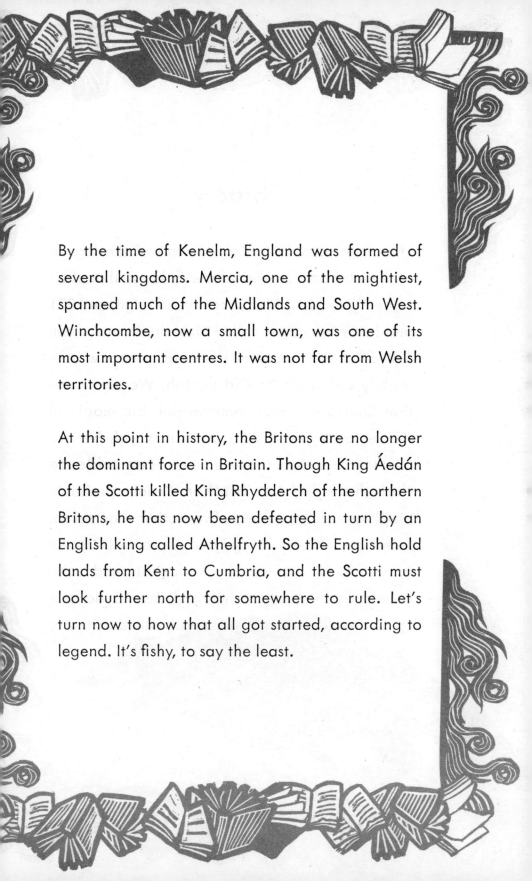

By the time of Kenelm, England was formed of several kingdoms. Mercia, one of the mightiest, spanned much of the Midlands and South West. Winchcombe, now a small town, was one of its most important centres. It was not far from Welsh territories.

At this point in history, the Britons are no longer the dominant force in Britain. Though King Áedán of the Scotti killed King Rhydderch of the northern Britons, he has now been defeated in turn by an English king called Athelfryth. So the English hold lands from Kent to Cumbria, and the Scotti must look further north for somewhere to rule. Let's turn now to how that all got started, according to legend. It's fishy, to say the least.

A CLOAK OF STARS

AND THE FIRST KING OF SCOTS

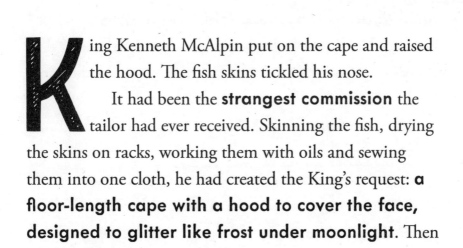

King Kenneth McAlpin put on the cape and raised the hood. The fish skins tickled his nose.

It had been the **strangest commission** the tailor had ever received. Skinning the fish, drying the skins on racks, working them with oils and sewing them into one cloth, he had created the King's request: **a floor-length cape with a hood to cover the face, designed to glitter like frost under moonlight**. Then he had delivered it to the castle.

Now the King's reflection shone back at him from the metal of a shield hanging on the wall. There he stood, Kenneth, son of Alpin, resplendent, glorious, destined for greatness. His own kin had brought Simon Brecc's throne from the Hill of Tara to their castle at Scone. And Kenneth's own backside had warmed the cold stone as his head received the ancient crown. Now he would ensure that **his future lived up to his past**, for all was not as it should be. The domains Kenneth had inherited were small, surrounded by territories claimed by Picts, Danes and Britons. If he was not careful, his kingdom would be swallowed like a grain of sand by the tide. He had to make war on his neighbours.

The only problem was that his **barons were too timid to do as they were told**. Each night for weeks, Kenneth had given his lords speeches of valour and conquest. Would they be the first since Scota to submit to foreign rule?

'Let's start with the Picts,' he said, 'and work out from there!'

Even so, **the barons were of one voice**: not even divine intervention – not even an angel sent by God, they declared – would make them change their minds. And that had given Kenneth his idea. And that was why he was now standing before his shield, dressed in fish-skin robes.

Leaving his room, Kenneth tiptoed through the moonlit castle, light reflecting off his cloak and dancing over the walls. The smell of fish was almost overwhelming. He stole into the first baron's chamber, opened his mouth and, in the voice he had been practising, began to speak.

'In the name of the Living God,' he said, somewhat

higher than he had meant to, then paused. The baron
was still sleeping. Kenneth cleared his throat. The fabric
**dangled from his raised arms like feathers and
shone with innumerable silver beams.**

'In the name of the Living God,' he repeated, more
loudly. The baron did not stir.

Kenneth clapped and the man jerked awake, his eyes
widening as they found the apparition. Then the King
flung out his arms again, and moonlight raced round the
walls.

'IN THE NAME OF THE LIVING GOD,' he sang in
a perfect, angelic wail, 'I ORDER YOU TO OBEY YOUR
KING'S COMMANDS AND AGREE TO DESTROY
THE PICTS.'

The baron did not move. His mouth hung open, and his eyes grew round in the dark. Then Kenneth stepped back into the shadows and slipped out of the door. **He visited all his barons that night, relaying the same message.**

The next day, they agreed to make war on their neighbours, each of them sharing the vision of an angel that they had received in the night. If any of them had seen through Kenneth's disguise, or noted a lingering smell of the harbour, they did not make it known.

When the invasions began, Kenneth was merciless, destroying the Pictish villages and towns, as well as their armies. And when raiders from Denmark weakened other Pictish strongholds, Kenneth crossed the mountains and subdued them altogether. In time, he, King of the Scotti, became ruler of Albany from the Forth to Orkney, and the greatest power in the north. And the loyalty from his men never faltered. He had caught them: hook, line and sinker.

History

Historically speaking, Scotland was established in the sixth century by an Irish tribe called the Dál Riada, which claimed territory on the north-west coast of Britain. The Latin name for the Irish was the Scotti, which is why the kingdom they established came to be known as Scotland.

Kenneth MacAlpin (Cináed Mac Ailpín), also known as Kenneth I, was a king of the Dál Riada and is said to have died in 858. He is **still seen as the founding father** of the Scottish royal dynasty.

One fifteenth-century Scottish chronicle tells us that Kenneth, hoping to convince his reluctant barons to make war on the surrounding kingdoms, crept around his castle at Scone performing an angelic message to each baron in turn. So that he would look like an angel, he wore a costume made entirely of shiny fish skins. Whether or not they were fooled, the King got his way.

STIRRINGS IN THE SAND

THE NORMAN CONQUEST AND THE RETURN OF GOGMAGOG

At the very start of things, Corineus wrestled Gogmagog and threw him into the sea. When the Trojans peered over the cliff edge, the great body was already out of sight. It was coming to rest, moon-eyed, on the seabed. But the giant was not dead and did not truly die as a thousand and more tides rose and fell. **He grew green and grey.** Particles of skin and sinew swelled and puckered with water and brine, but some force resisted rot and the giant's heart went on flickering in his chest.

While Gogmagog slept, Hiber's fleet sailed by and Bladud fell from the sky on to the Temple of Apollo, but then, from deep below the earth, **a demon ascended and possessed the body of the giant.**

Now fish darted more quickly over him and deep sand swirled that had rested for an age. Gogmagog opened his eyes and balled up his wrinkled hands.

You might have noticed a churning in the waves as he stood, then a swell in the current making progress west, along the Cornish coast, round the southernmost part of Britain. That was Gogmagog, walking beneath the flow, his head warmed by the sun.

Perhaps he ascended at the mouth of the Severn, where the mud would have dragged at his ancient legs and seabirds would have spiralled in flocks around him, feeding him by the handful. Or perhaps he crawled, swollen, up the cliffs of Ceredigion, his skin taking on the colours of the rock. He walked on till he found the place where he had long ago **hidden a stash of ancestral treasure**. Gogmagog crawled on to that gold and slept, covering his kelp-haired head, until a human king found the hill and built a fortress there called Castell Dinas Bran.

On the night of the disaster, the fortress's hall was full, and the songs and ale were flowing. The sleeping Gogmagog was awoken and the malice within him rose.

He destroyed Castell Dinas Bran, gorging on blood and bone, leaving none of its people alive. Then he occupied the ruins and **many diabolical creatures joined him**. They raided the ancient treasury on which he had been sleeping, bringing out idols cast in gold: peacocks,

horses, swans and oxen finely worked; gigantic gods that glistered and hungered for flesh. The greatest was a bull cast of gold around which, beside the castle, the resurrected Gogmagog built a city and encircled it with high walls and deep trenches. In that snare for souls, he held tournaments and fairs, and the demons of that place conjured flags and streamers, as well as the din of trade and revelry and the aromas of delicious food. These poured down the hillside, and passing travellers were lured through the gates. Once they went inside the city walls, **they would never be seen again**.

Time passed and, as it did, much of the land that had belonged to the Trojans fell to Saxon and Scottish kings, and devilry thrived. But soon the saints came and spread the word of God, baptising people in the name of Christ. When a church was built nearby, the demons went into hiding. But still they did not disappear. **Their influence remained** like a dark mist over Castell Dinas Bran, and people would not go near it.

But now, a conqueror called William was advancing across the sea. He was not a giant, but time has made him one. On a field in Hastings, in the year 1066, an arrow fell from the sky, entered his rival's head and blinded him. The rival was called Harold and he had been King of England.

William took the throne, then his armies marched on Wales. As they entered that wild domain, they met an old Briton who spoke of the monsters that had guarded Castell Dinas Bran. He said they were still up there, lying in evil wait.

At this, William's young cousin, Payn, addressed the King. 'Let me go to the hill', he said, seizing his shield. 'Let me take on the giant.'

As a child, Payn had sought out stories of war and adventure that would help him become a warrior. He had practised jousting with hobby horses and wooden lances. As a teenager, he had exercised every day: fencing, riding, lifting. He had done this so that one day, when he was a knight, he would prove his nobility. **Now his moment had come.**

With King William's agreement, Payn Peverill gathered fifteen knights and an army of soldiers. They made for Castell Dinas Bran in the wind and growing darkness. The hill on which it rested was smooth and steep, the valleys beyond it perilous. Freezing water ran in rivulets, exposing stone beneath the turf. Up the troop went, tripping in the mud, wiping rain from their eyebrows, the light of the invisible sun dimming behind the clouds and night falling fast around them.

No fires could be lit because of the rain, and the

soldiers' sodden tunics chilled them to the bone. They crouched among the ruins, where the wind was least strong, though everywhere it was strengthening. Suddenly there was a flash of lightning and, following it in a heartbeat, a violent clap of thunder. The wind roared and a storm lit up the sky for as far as the eye could see. As the clouds erupted, the **men dived to the ground, covering their heads**. Payn tried to shout words of comfort over the noise, but it was no use. This was no ordinary storm. **The Devil himself was in the clouds, entering their minds.** Payn gripped the handle of his great shield more tightly and sheltered beneath its gilding. Gusting out of the darkness was more than ice and wind: all the sickness of an evil world was raining from the sky. What use were his weapons against such an onslaught? What use was his strength and training? And in the privacy of the darkness, for all his strength and training, Payn Peverill began to cry.

Underneath his shield, where he could hear his own small voice, he tried to recall something to bring him comfort. He wished he was back **with his mother, safe in one of her loving hugs**. But he was not. He was with his friends and if he did not defend them now, then they would all die. Gripping his sword, he prayed a flutter of words. Then there was a roar even louder than the thunder and Payn Peverill stood up, **lifting his face with more courage than he felt**, determined to face whatever now stood before him.

Gogmagog's altered form, possessed, demonic and terrifying, stood silhouetted against the sky. In his hand he held a club: an oak tree, ripped up by the roots. His chest swelled and contracted like the heaving sea, smoke billowed from his nostrils and fire belched from his mouth. The bright glare of those flames bleached the ruined walls and exposed the cowering groups of soldiers. But Payn forced himself to stand tall.

He crossed himself, trembling, as the giant raised the club. But as soon as the cross was formed, Gogmagog found he could not bring the club down. Payn shouted over the wind, 'Who are you?'

The demon bellowed through the giant's cavernous mouth. **His voice felt like an earthquake.** 'I am from Hell. I have found the giants' treasure and I have occupied their land.'

'Where is the treasure?' cried Payn, although the noise of the storm was lessening.

'Nowhere destined for you to find.'

Then a stench met Payn's nostrils, so terrible that the

soldiers around him vomited on the grass. He saw that
Gogmagog's great grey face was slackening and his
eyes were becoming dim. The club slipped from his
hand and men fled to escape it as it crashed to the
ground. Then the body swayed and fell, **smashing
against the ruins, scattering more soldiers
and collapsing on to the hillside**. As the wind
dropped, the stench and the clouds began to fade.
And Payn could not believe that he was still alive
or that the men around him were safe. As the stone
walls sparkled in the first rays of dawn, he crossed
himself again, because he knew that it was this sign
that had saved him.

Together, as a beautiful sunrise pooled over the
hill, the soldiers lifted Gogmagog's ruined body
and carried it back to King William. He had a
great pit dug in the nearby town of Llangollen,
into which they laid the giant and covered
him with soil. In reward for his bravery, Payn
received lands thereabouts, while the huge club
was kept by the King as a trophy of his conquest.
Still, Gogmagog's treasure never could be found.

After that, the Normans ruled, and in time they called themselves English and began to speak the English tongue. In Wales, Brutus's people took the red dragon as their flag and kept the language of Brutus, Cordelia and Lludd. In Scotland, the descendants of Scota prized freedom, just as Gaythelos had done. More peoples came and went than Merlin could ever have foreseen. The earth consumed Gogmagog and the water absorbed the earth, **till his flesh was inside every leaf and rock of Albion**.

History

After William the Conqueror was conceived, his mother had a dream that she was giving birth to a tree. Its shadow reached across the plains of Normandy in France and out over England. She understood that **the tree represented her unborn son.** She understood that he would rule not only Normandy, but England too. Her dream came true. When he grew up, he would lead the Norman Conquest of England.

In the early part of 1066, the year in which the Norman Conquest took place, England's king, Edward the Confessor, died without an heir. His brother-in-law, Harold Godwinson, thought he should inherit the throne. Over the sea, William, the Duke of Normandy and descendant of Edward's mother, disagreed. He thought it should be him. After Harold had held the throne for a few months, William met him on a battlefield in Hastings in southern England, defeated him and seized the throne.

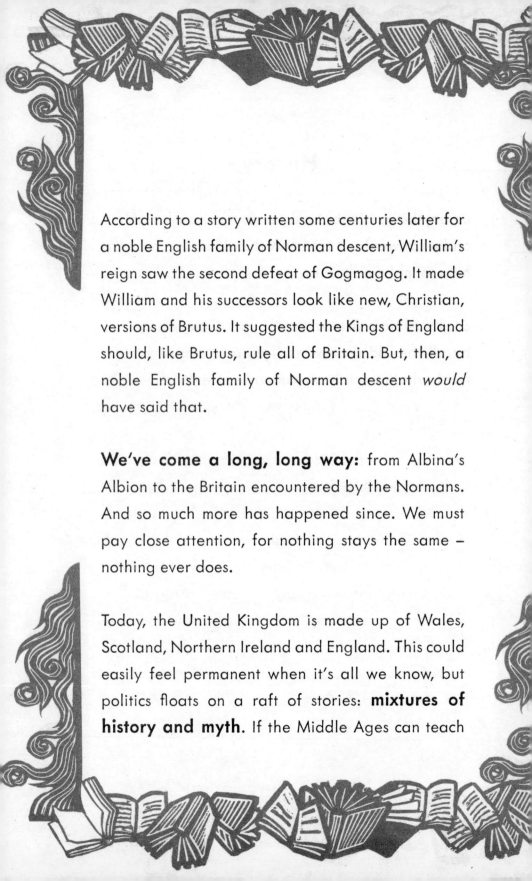

According to a story written some centuries later for a noble English family of Norman descent, William's reign saw the second defeat of Gogmagog. It made William and his successors look like new, Christian, versions of Brutus. It suggested the Kings of England should, like Brutus, rule all of Britain. But, then, a noble English family of Norman descent *would* have said that.

We've come a long, long way: from Albina's Albion to the Britain encountered by the Normans. And so much more has happened since. We must pay close attention, for nothing stays the same – nothing ever does.

Today, the United Kingdom is made up of Wales, Scotland, Northern Ireland and England. This could easily feel permanent when it's all we know, but politics floats on a raft of stories: **mixtures of history and myth**. If the Middle Ages can teach

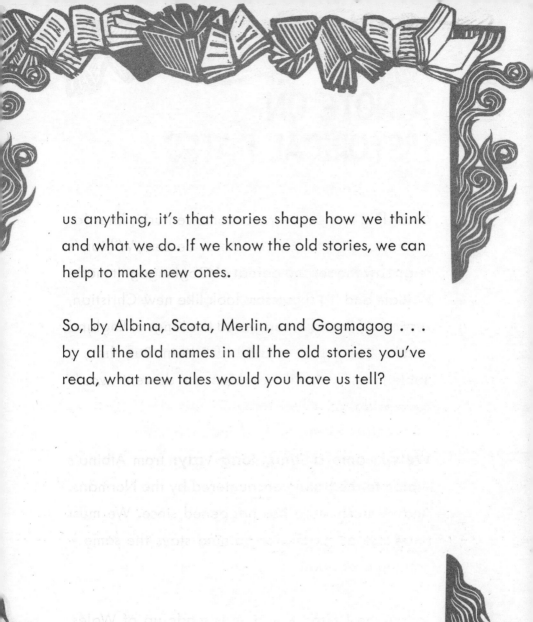

us anything, it's that stories shape how we think and what we do. If we know the old stories, we can help to make new ones.

So, by Albina, Scota, Merlin, and Gogmagog . . . by all the old names in all the old stories you've read, what new tales would you have us tell?

A NOTE ON HISTORICAL DATES

BC/AD

In the medieval Christian mind, all history before Christ's birth (BC) belonged to dark, ancient times. The passing years of the post-Christ era, however, from the very first *Anno Domini* (AD), Year of our Lord, were counted as we count them now. You might sometimes see the terms BCE (Before Common Era) and CE (Common Era) – these mean the same thing but are more religiously neutral.

GLOSSARY OF KEY FIGURES AND PLACES

KEY FIGURES

Albina: Syrian princess who founds Albion.

Aeneas: Leader of the Trojans after the Fall of Troy.

Albanac: Son of Brutus and Inogen, King of Albany.

Albina: Syrian princess who founds Albion.

Argentille: Queen of Norfolk and Lindsey, wife of Havelok.

Aurelius Ambrosius: King of Britain, older brother of Uther Pendragon, uncle of King Arthur.

Bladud: Founder of Bath, inventor who attempts flight and father of Lear.

Brutus: Founder of Britain, great grandson of Aeneas, descendant of Venus.

Cafall: King Arthur's hound, associated with a legendary pawprint on a stone (now missing) on the summit of the hill Carngafallt in Mid Wales.

Corineus: First lord of Cornwall and killer of Gogmagog.

Diana: Roman goddess of the hunt, who prophesies to Brutus that he will establish his kingdom on an island in the western ocean.

Estrildis: German princess captured by King Humber, imprisoned by King Locrin and killed by Corineus's daughter, Gwendolen. Mother of Sabrina.

Gaythelos: Greek prince who becomes the husband of Scota and first king of the Scotti.

Gogmagog: Leader of the giants of Albion.

GLOSSARY

Grim: Refugee founder of Grimsby, formerly a knight in the court of King Gunter of Denmark.

Gwendolen: Daughter of Corineus and third ever monarch of Britain.

Gwendydd: Queen of the Northern Britons, prophetess, wife of Rhydderch, sister of Merlin.

Havelok: King of Denmark, husband of Argentille. Stepson of Grim.

Hengist: Descendant of Woden, leader of the Saxons who establish kingdoms in Britain during the reign of Vortigern.

Herleva: Historical mother of William the Conqueror, though little is known about her. Daughter of tanners.

Hiber: Son of Scota and Gaythelos, who gives his name to Hibernia (later Ireland).

Humber: King of the Huns, who gives his name to the Humber Estuary.

Igraine: British noblewoman, mother of King Arthur and wife of Uther Pendragon.

Inogen: Greek princess who Brutus takes as his queen.

Kamber: Son of Brutus and Inogen, King of Kambria.

Kenelm: Semi-historical child saint, killed at the orders of his jealous sister, Quendryda.

Kenneth McAlpin: Cináed Mac Ailpín (died 858), historical ruler of the Dál Riada, remembered in legend as the first Scottish king.

Lear: Founder of Leicester, son of Bladud, protagonist of Shakespeare's play *King Lear*.

Lludd: King of Britain who, helped by his brother, rids the land of three plagues.

GLOSSARY

Locrin: Son of Brutus and Inogen, King of Loegria.

Merlin: Boy with no human father who comes to be a soothsayer and magician for kings Vortigern, Aurelius Ambrosius, Uther and Arthur. Responsible for the transportation of Stonehenge from Ireland to Amesbury, he spends time in the court of King Rhydderch in his old age, as well as the forests of Calidon. Brother of Gwendydd.

Mungo: Patron saint of Glasgow, died 614, also known as Kentigern. Historical but found in many legends.

Payn Peverill: Legendary cousin of William the Conqueror, who defeats Gogmagog on Castell Dinas Bran.

Rhydderch: King of the Northern Britons when Merlin is an old man.

Sabrina: Daughter of Estrildis and Locrin, who gives her name to the River Severn.

Scota: Egyptian princess who becomes the first queen of the Scotti. Daughter of the biblical Pharaoh Rameses II.

Scotti: People who come to populate Hibernia (later Ireland) and who will become the Scots.

Sif : One of the Norse goddesses, presented in some sources as a mortal queen of Thrace.

Simon Brecc: King of the Scotti in Spain, who travels to Hibernia and discovers a throne of destiny.

Taliesin: Prophet and bard who stays with Merlin and Gwendydd in the forests of Calidon.

Uther Pendragon: King of Britain, younger brother of Aurelius Ambrosius, husband of Igraine and father of King Arthur.

Venus: Roman goddess of love and ancestor of Brutus.

Vortigern: Britain's worst king, who unjustly seizes the throne from King Constans, older brother of Aurelius Ambrosius, and lets the Saxons, led by Hengist, into the land.

William the Conqueror: Historical Duke of Normandy who became King of England after leading the 1066 Norman Conquest of England.

Woden Norse: All-Father god, presented in some sources as a mortal king who founds kingdoms in the north and is a descendant of Sif. Hengist is one of Woden's descendants.

KEY PLACES

Albany: The territory that becomes Scotland, named after Brutus's and Inogen's son Albanac.

Albion: Name given to Britain before it was called Britain.

Bath: City in south-west England built over

thermal springs and founded, according to legend, by King Bladud.

Brigantia: Now called A Coruña, the Spanish coastal town founded by Scota and Gaythelos, where they built the Tower of Hercules.

Britain: Name given to an island in the western ocean by Brutus, where he founds a New Troy and a royal dynasty.

Calidon/Caledonian Forest: Ancient forest that once covered large swathes of Scotland. The place where, according to legend, Merlin lives out his old age, along with his sister, Gwendydd.

Carngafallt: Hill in Radnorshire, Mid Wales, associated with a legend about a footprint left by King Arthur's dog, Cafall.

Castell Dinas Bran: Thirteenth-century hilltop castle above Llangollen in

Denbighshire, Wales, associated in legend with the story of the second defeat of Gogmagog by Payn Peverill.

Dál Riada: Fifth- to ninth-century Gaelic kingdom that would extend from Ireland into northern Britain, later becoming the Kingdom of Alba, later Scotland.

Dameliock: Prehistoric site in Cornwall also known as Tregeare Rounds hill fort. According to legend, the site of the Duke of Cornwall's other castle, where he meets Uther's army and is killed.

Dart: River up which Brutus and his fleet are said to have sailed when reaching Britain.

Dinas Emrys: Hill beside Yr Wyddfa (Snowdon) where, according to legend, Vortigern tries to build his tower, the child Merlin makes his first prophecies and the red and white dragons hidden by Lludd are re-discovered.

Dinas Ffaraon Dandde: The name for Dinas Emrys before Merlin makes his prophecies there. The place where Lludd, according to legend, hides two dragons.

Gaul: A vast western European territory covering those of modern-day France, Belgium, the Netherlands, as well as parts of other neighbouring countries.

Giants' Dance: Mythical name for Stonehenge, before it was carried from Hibernia to Britain.

Glasgow: City in Lanarkshire in southern Scotland, associated in legend with the court of King Rhydderch and the church of St Mungo.

Gogmagog's Leap: Site of Gogmagog's legendary wrestling match with Corineus, associated with Plymouth Hoe.

Grimsby: Town on the Humber Estuary, which, legend has it, was founded by Grim.

GLOSSARY

Hibernia: The name given to Ireland by Hiber, son of Scota and Gaythelos.

Humber Estuary: Major estuary on the north-east coast of England, named, according to legend, after Humber, King of the Huns.

Kambria: The territory that becomes Wales, named after Brutus's and Inogen's son Kamber.

Loegria: The territory that becomes England, named after Brutus's and Inogen's son Locrin.

Ludgate: Area of London said to have been named in memory of King Lludd.

New Troy: Legendary name for the city founded by Brutus, which is renamed London in the reign of King Lludd.

Plymouth Hoe: Raised area of land beside the sea in the Devonshire city of Plymouth, England.

River Severn: Longest river in Britain, reaching the sea near Bristol. Mythical resting place of Estrildis and Sabrina, who gave it her name.

Scone: Town in Perth and Kinross, Scotland, where Kenneth McAlpin is said to have dressed as an angel to persuade his barons to make war against the Picts.

Springs of Galabes: Mythical place to which Merlin retreats after Vortigern's death.

Stonehenge: Prehistoric stone monument near Amesbury on Salisbury Plain, England. Mythical resting place of Britons massacred by the Saxons, as well as King Arthur's uncle and father, King Aurelius Ambrosius and King Uther Pendragon.

Thrace: Ancient territory touching modern-day Bulgaria, Greece and Turkey.

Tintagel: Coastal, clifftop castle in north Cornwall belonging, according to legend, to

Gorlois, Duke of Cornwall, and where Uther disguised himself as Gorlois so he could visit the Duke's wife, Igraine.

Totnes: The Devonshire town where, according to legend, Brutus docked his fleet when he first arrived in Britain.

Tower of Hercules: First-century Roman lighthouse in A Coruña, Spain, attributed in Scottish myths to Scota and Gaythelos.

Troy: A ncient city shrouded in legend, populated by Trojans, said to have been captured by the Greeks.

Winchcombe: Town in Gloucestershire, England, and setting for the legend of Kenelm and Quendryda.

Winchester: City in southern England where, according to legend, Aurelius Ambrosius dies.

Yr Wyddfa: Snowdon, the tallest mountain in Wales.

EMAIN
SIMON BRECC
ARGENTILLE & HAVELOK
GRIM
PAYN PEVERILL
VORTIGERN
CORDELIA & LEAR
SCOTA & GAYTHELOS
CAFALL
KENELM
SABRINA
LLUDD & DRAGONS
the NEW TROY
BLADUD
JOSEPH of ARIMATHEA
STONE-HENGE
IGRAINE & ARTHUR
HENGIST & HORSA
BRUTUS & the TROJANS
CORINEUS WRESTLES GOGMAGOG

ACKNOWLEDGEMENTS

My thanks go to Anna Martin, Samuel Perrett,
Alison Padley and all the team at Hachette
Children's Group. I've learned so much!

To all at Georgina Capel Associates,
thank you for your daring.

Alex Mirza, thank you for printing my illustrations
when I was too great with child to reach the
press. And thank you Chris Pig, the most flexible
printmaker in the West.

To my family and to Laura, thank you.

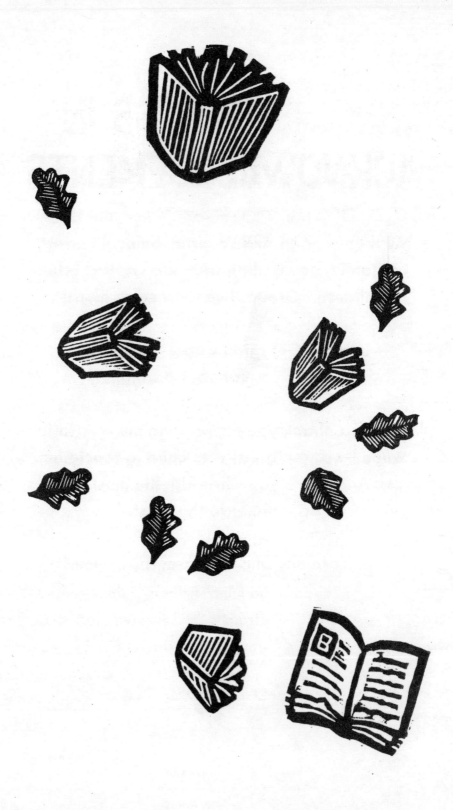

STORYLAND